COOK
fast
EAT
well

Many thanks to my wonderful family, Adam, Ruby, and Ben, for the constant flow of hot tea and encouragement to get this book completed.

Huge gratitude is also due to the team that made the jigsaw fit together so beautifully: Alice Cannan, Deirdre Rooney, Helen McTeer and Anna Osborn. As ever, enormous thanks go to Catie Ziller for trusting me with this challenging but ultimately hugely rewarding project.

SUE QUINN

COOK
fast
EAT
well

5 INGREDIENTS
10 MINUTES
160 RECIPES

STERLING EPICURE
New York

CONTENTS

INTRODUCTION

Finding the time to prepare delicious food is a challenge for most of us, whether or not we enjoy cooking. Many cookbooks and television cooking shows would have us think that tasty meals necessarily involve long lists of ingredients and several hours' commitment in the kitchen. During the process of devising and testing the recipes for this book I realised how wrong this is. I was amazed at how little time it takes to prepare wonderful plates of food with a handful of ingredients; complex and arduous definitely doesn't mean tastier.

One key to super-quick cooking is well-chosen ingredients. Fresh pasta, jars of marinated vegetables, frozen fruit, punchy sauces, canned tomatoes and excellent bouillon cubes or bouillon powders are all perfectly acceptable shortcut ingredients that enable you to cook speedily without compromising quality or flavor.

Another key to speedy cooking is organization. Cooking time starts once all your ingredients and cooking utensils are assembled—I urge you to do this before you start each recipe. Be sure to follow the method as instructed, as multi-tasking is often required, but use your judgement. If, for example, you have an induction cooktop that can boil water exceptionally quickly, use this method instead of boiling the water to cook pasta on your electric or gas range.

Finally, remember that everyone cooks at a different speed. All these dishes can be made in 10 minutes or less, if you work quickly, but don't worry if it takes a little longer to start with. Once you get into the swing of speedy cooking you will have a repertoire of meals that can be whipped up more quickly than you ever thought possible.

An ideal pantry for super-quick cooking

BASICS

- Oil (olive and vegetable)
- Sea salt (flakes and fine)
- Black peppercorns
- Sugar (soft light brown, superfine, and muscovado)
- Butter
- Bread (country and baguette)
- Eggs
- Good-quality bouillon cubes/ bouillon powder or liquid stock
- Nuts and seeds
- Spices (smoked paprika, cumin, chili flakes, cayenne pepper)
- Dried fruit
- Noodles (fresh and dried)
- Fresh pasta
- Couscous

FRESH

- Garlic
- Herbs
- Lemons/limes
- Scallions
- Chiles
- Tomatoes

DAIRY

- Greek-style yogurt
- Crème fraîche
- Cream
- Cream cheese
- Cheese (parmesan, feta, mozzarella, cheddar, goat, halloumi, mascarpone)

FISH

- Smoked fish (salmon and mackerel)

MEAT

- Bacon

CANS AND JARS

- Pulses (chickpeas, lentils, and beans)
- Fish (tuna, anchovies, and sardines)
- Vegetables in oil (sundried tomatoes, grilled eggplant, bell peppers, and artichokes)
- Capers
- Olives

OTHERS

- Flour tortillas
- Popcorn
- Ready-to-eat (precooked) grains, such as quinoa, farro, or a mixture
- Chocolate spread

PASTES, SAUCES AND DIPS

- Curry paste
- Pesto
- Tomato sauce
- Hummus
- Chili sauce (Tabasco®, Sriracha, and sweet chili)
- Harissa paste
- Soy sauce
- Mustard
- Mayonnaise

FROZEN

- Fruit
- Vegetables

CHAPTER I

plates to share & light bites

SWEET SPICED
pumpkin SEEDS

makes 1 cup (4½ oz/130 g) / preparation : 5 minutes + 5 minutes cooling
equipment : bowl, heavy frying pan, 1 sheet parchment paper

4½ oz (130 g/1 cup)
pumpkin seeds

**3 tablespoons
soft light brown
sugar**

**1½ teaspoons
ground cumin**

**¾ teaspoon
cayenne pepper**

**1½ teaspoons
sweet smoked paprika**

Combine all the ingredients in the bowl and stir. Heat 1 teaspoon vegetable oil in the frying pan and add the seed mixture. Cook, stirring constantly, for 1–2 minutes, or until the sugar has caramelized and the pumpkin seeds start to pop. Spread out on the parchment paper and allow to cool.

PARMESAN *popcorn*

serves 4 as a snack / preparation : 5 minutes
equipment : cheese grater, small pan, large heavy lidded pan

1 oz (30 g)
parmesan
cheese

1 oz (30 g)
salted butter

2 oz (50 g/
¼ cup)
popcorn
kernels

Finely grate the parmesan. Melt the butter in the small pan. Pour the corn into the large pan and add 1 tablespoon vegetable oil. Stir to coat, then cover.

Set over medium—high heat. When the first kernel of corn pops, remove the pan from the heat for 1 minute, covered, then return to the heat. Frequently shake the pan as the corn pops. When the popping slows down—after about 2 minutes—remove from the heat and leave for 1 minute with the lid on. Add the parmesan, butter, and fine sea salt to taste, stirring well to coat. Serve warm.

kale CHIPS

serves 4 as a snack / preparation : 10 minutes + 5 minutes cooling
equipment : large and small bowl, baking sheet lined with parchment paper

3½ oz (100 g) kale leaves

½ teaspoon smoked paprika

I teaspoon sugar

Preheat the oven to 350°F (180°C). Remove any large stalks from the kale and break into bite-sized pieces if the leaves are large. Place in the bowl, add I tablespoon olive oil, and toss with your hands to coat.

Combine the sugar, paprika, and ½ teaspoon sea salt in a small bowl. Add bit by bit to the kale, tossing well as you go. Spread out on the baking sheet and bake for 5 minutes, or until crisp and starting to brown at the edges. Let the kale cool and crisp up for 5 minutes before serving.

FRIED PADRÓN *peppers* WITH TOGARASHI

serves 4 as a snack / preparation : 8 minutes
equipment : large heavy frying pan, paper towels

Togarashi chili pepper, for sprinkling

9 oz (250 g) Padrón peppers

Wash the peppers and dry them thoroughly. Heat 3 tablespoons olive oil in the frying pan until very hot. Carefully add the peppers and turn to coat in the oil. Cook for 3–4 minutes, shaking frequently, until they start to blister and the skin turns brown in patches. Don't overcook. Remove and drain on paper towels. Serve immediately, sprinkled with togarashi.

<u>NOTE</u> Beware of the occasional very hot pepper.

parmesan LACE CRACKERS

serves 4 as a snack / preparation : 5 minutes + 5 minutes cooling
equipment : cheese grater, bowl, baking sheet lined with parchment paper, wire rack

2 oz (50 g) parmesan cheese

1 teaspoon poppy seeds

Preheat the oven to 400°F (200°C). Finely grate the parmesan into the bowl. Add the poppy seeds and mix well. Place heaping tablespoons of the mixture onto the baking sheet and flatten out with the back of a spoon.

Bake for 3 minutes or until pale gold. Leave on the baking sheet for a couple of minutes then slide onto a wire rack to cool and crisp up.

GARLIC *tortilla* CHIPS

makes 16 / preparation : 8 minutes + 5 minutes cooling
equipment : baking sheet, garlic press, small bowl, pastry brush

2 garlic cloves

2 flour tortillas

Preheat the oven to 400°F (200°C) and slide the baking sheet in while it gets hot. Meanwhile, crush the garlic into the bowl and add 1 tablespoon olive oil. Stir. Brush the tortillas with the garlicky oil on both sides and sprinkle with sea salt flakes. Cut each tortilla into 8 wedges.

Remove the baking sheet from the oven and place the tortillas on it. Bake for 5–6 minutes until pale gold. Slide onto a wire rack to cool and crisp up.

taramasalata

serves 4 / preparation : 5 minutes
equipment : small bowl, food processor or blender

3½ fl oz (100 ml)
extra virgin olive oil

7 oz (200 g) smoked
cod roe (caviar spread)

3½ fl oz
(100 ml)
milk

2 oz (60 g)
stale white
bread

3 tablespoons
lemon juice

Remove the crusts from the bread, tear into pieces and place in the bowl. Add the milk and let the bread soak.

Place the roe in the blender with the soaked bread. Blend until smooth.

With the motor running, very slowly pour in the extra virgin olive oil, then the lemon juice. Add more lemon juice to taste, or more water, if too thick. Serve with carrot sticks and bread.

guacamole

serves 4 as a dip / preparation : 5 minutes
equipment : bowl, garlic press

**Tabasco® sauce
(to taste)**

**2 large ripe
avocados**

**I ripe
tomato**

**I garlic
clove**

**I tablespoon
lime juice**

Scoop the avocado flesh into a bowl and mash roughly with a fork. Crush the garlic into the bowl and add the lime juice, salt and pepper, and Tabasco sauce to taste. Mix.

Finely chop the tomato and gently fold it into the avocado mixture. Taste for seasoning and add more salt, pepper, lime juice, or Tabasco to taste. Serve with chopped raw vegetables.

black bean
AND HARISSA DIP

serves 4 as a snack / preparation : 5 minutes
equipment : food processor

I can black
beans, about
7 oz (200 g)
drained weight

A squeeze of
lime

I teaspoon
harissa paste

A small handful of
cilantro leaves, plus
extra for sprinkling

Drain the beans, reserving the liquid. Blend the beans in a food processor with the cilantro, harissa paste, and lime juice together with 2 tablespoons olive oil. Add 1–2 tablespoons of reserved can liquid and process to the desired consistency. Add salt and pepper and more lime juice to taste.

Spoon into a serving dish and sprinkle with cilantro leaves. Serve with lime wedges and tortilla chips.

fava bean AND
SESAME DIP

serves 4 as a starter / preparation : 10 minutes
equipment : saucepan, blender or food processor

4 garlic
cloves

½ teaspoon
soy sauce

1 teaspoon
sesame oil

2 tablespoons
lime juice

1 lb 2 oz (500 g)
frozen fava beans

Fill the saucepan with water and bring it to a boil. Meanwhile, peel the garlic cloves. Cook the fava beans and garlic cloves in the boiling water for about 4 minutes, or until the beans are tender. Drain. Transfer to the blender or food processor and add the sesame oil, lime juice, and soy sauce.

Measure out 6 fl oz (180 ml/¾ cup) cold water. With the motor running, gradually add enough water to form a smooth and creamy dip. Season with salt and pepper. Serve with chopped raw vegetables.

tomato AND
BASIL BRUSCHETTA

makes 4 / preparation : 10 minutes
equipment : baking sheet, bowl

4 ripe roma (plum) tomatoes

4 baguette slices, cut on the diagonal

1 garlic clove

8 basil leaves

Turn on the broiler. Arrange the baguette slices on the baking sheet, drizzle lightly with olive oil and toast on both sides until golden. Meanwhile, finely dice the tomatoes and tear the basil. Combine in a bowl with 1 tablespoon olive oil and salt and pepper. Peel the garlic, cut it in half, and rub over the toasted bread. Top with the tomato mixture.

bruschetta VARIATIONS

makes 8
For something different, try one of these variations
on the Tomato and basil bruschetta
recipe on pages 32–33

olive oil

A handful of mixed
soft herbs such
as basil, oregano,
chives, parsley, and
thyme

3 tablespoons
plain yogurt

I eggplant

½ teaspoon
cayenne
pepper

8 tablespoons
soft goat cheese

I garlic clove

MIXED HERBS AND GOAT CHEESE

Finely chop the herbs, combine with the goat cheese and stir until creamy. Spread generously over toasted baguette slices, rubbed with garlic.

FRIED SPICED EGGPLANT AND YOGURT

Cut the eggplant into small dice and fry in 2 tablespoons olive oil. Add the cayenne pepper and salt and pepper. Cook, stirring, until tender. Meanwhile, crush the garlic and mix with the yogurt. Spoon the eggplant onto toasted baguette slices and top with a spoonful of the garlicky yogurt.

1 tablespoon capers

4 tablespoons butter

3 oz (80 g/⅓ cup) sundried tomato paste

A handful of black olives

7 oz (200 g) mushrooms

2 garlic cloves

10 oregano leaves

SUNDRIED TOMATO, OLIVE AND OREGANO

Mix the sundried tomato paste with the oregano leaves (chopped) and a splash of extra virgin olive oil to loosen. Spread over toasted baguette slices and top with black olives (sliced).

MUSHROOMS AND CAPERS

Melt the butter in a frying pan and add the mushrooms (chopped). Mince the garlic and chop the capers, and add to the pan. Sauté, stirring, for 5 minutes. Season with salt and pepper. Spoon over toasted baguette slices.

bruschetta VARIATIONS

makes 8
For something different, try one of these variations
on the Tomato and basil bruschetta
recipe on pages 32–33

I small bunch of mint leaves

I jalapeño or other medium–hot chili pepper

A squeeze of lemon juice

I tablespoon lime juice

5½ oz (150 g) tuna loin

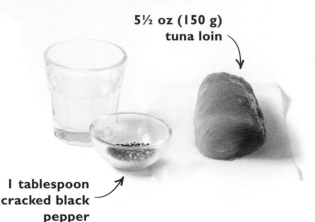

Bocconcini, for topping

I tablespoon cracked black pepper

BOCCONCINI, MINT, AND CHILI

In a mortar or blender, pound or process the mint leaves and the jalapeño (chopped) or other medium–hot chili pepper. Add 3 tablespoons olive oil, a squeeze of lemon, and stir. Top toasted baguette slices with bocconcini halves and drizzle with the mint and chili mixture.

TUNA CARPACCIO AND LIME

Heat a frying pan until smoking hot. Roll the tuna loin in the cracked black pepper. Sear for 10 seconds on each side, then slice very thinly. Whisk the lime juice and ½ tablespoon olive oil together. Arrange the tuna over toasted baguette slices, top with micro-greens and drizzle with the dressing.

I teaspoon dry sherry

I tablespoon heavy cream

½ red chili pepper

Ricotta cheese, for spreading

2½ oz (70 g) cavolo nero kale

3½ oz (100 g) butter

9 oz (250 g) chicken livers

2 garlic cloves

CAVOLO NERO KALE AND GARLIC

Finely slice the kale and sauté in 3 tablespoons olive oil for 2 minutes. Finely slice the garlic cloves and the red chili pepper and add to the pan. Generously season with salt and pepper. Gently cook for 5 minutes more. Spread toasted baguette slices with ricotta and top with kale.

CHICKEN LIVER PÂTÉ

Melt the butter. Fry the chicken livers in 1 tablespoon of the butter for 3 minutes. Blend in a food processor with the remaining butter, the cream, and salt and pepper. Stir in the sherry and taste for seasoning. Chill for about 30 minutes and then spread the paté generously over toasted baguette slices.

fishcakes WITH
DIPPING SAUCE

makes 12 / preparation : 10 minutes
equipment : food processor, heavy frying pan

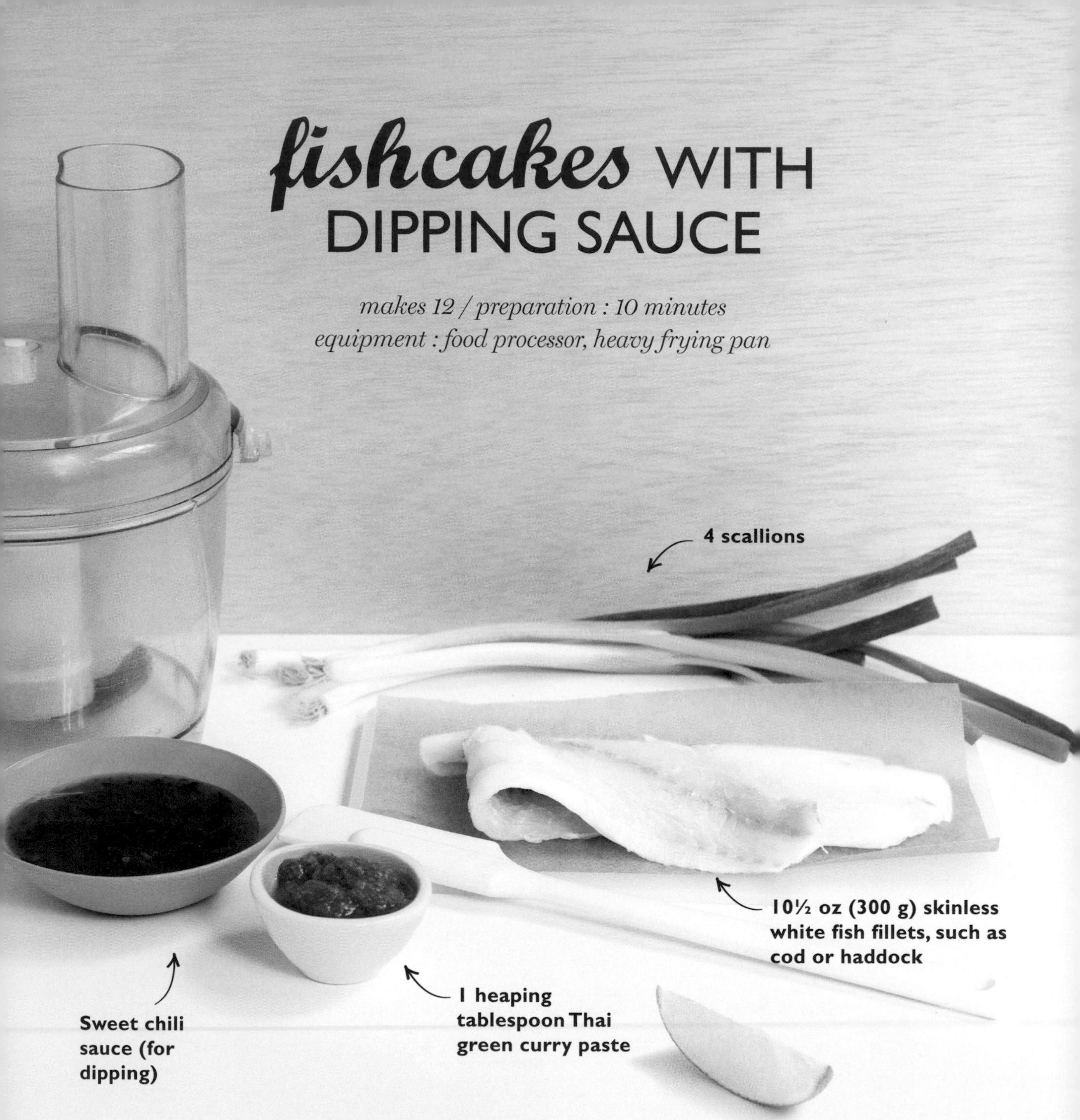

4 scallions

10½ oz (300 g) skinless white fish fillets, such as cod or haddock

Sweet chili sauce (for dipping)

I heaping tablespoon Thai green curry paste

Quarters of lime

Roughly chop the fish fillets and scallions. Place in the food processor, add the curry paste, and blend until almost smooth.

Roll tablespoons of the fish mixture into balls and flatten into patties. Heat 2 tablespoons vegetable oil in the heavy frying pan and fry the patties over medium–high heat for 1½–2 minutes on each side until golden. Serve hot with sweet chlli sauce for dipping and lime wedges on the side.

STICKY *chorizo* AND BEANS

serves 2 as a starter or tapas / preparation : 8 minutes
equipment : frying pan, colander

9 oz (250 g) chorizo

2 tablespoons honey

14 oz (400 g) can cannellini beans

1 tablespoon sherry vinegar

Heat 1 teaspoon olive oil in a frying pan. Meanwhile, remove the skin from the chorizo and slice into ½ inch (1 cm) rounds. Fry over medium–high heat for 4 minutes until crisp on the outside.

Meanwhile, drain and rinse the beans. Add the vinegar and honey to the chorizo pan, stirring as the mixture bubbles up. Reduce the heat, add the cannellini beans and cook, stirring, until warmed through. Season with salt and pepper.

zucchini AND NOODLE FRITTATA

serves 4 / preparation : 10 minutes
equipment : bowl, 8 inch (20 cm) non-stick frying pan, large plate

5½ oz (150 g) fresh rice noodles
(or leftover cooked pasta)

I small
zucchini

2 oz (50 g)
cheddar
cheese

3 eggs

Crack the eggs into a bowl and grate in the cheese. Stir. Finely slice the zucchini. Gently fry in 2 tablespoons olive oil for 2 minutes, or until tender. Add the noodles and cook, stirring, for 1 minute more. Pour into the bowl with the eggs and stir. Wipe out the frying pan, add 2 tablespoons olive oil, and pour in the egg and noodle mixture.

Cook over medium–high heat until golden underneath and starting to set on top. Invert onto the plate, then slide back into the frying pan. Cook for 1 more minute, or until just cooked through. Serve immediately.

WARM *goat cheese* WITH HONEY

serves 2 to 4 / preparation : 5 minutes
equipment : frying pan, shallow bowl, egg slice, absorbent paper towels

4 tablespoons honey

1 egg

1 tablespoon all-purpose flour

4 tablespoons pine nuts

7 oz (200 g) firm goat cheese

Heat ¼ inch (5 mm) olive oil In the frying pan until very hot. Meanwhile, lightly beat the egg in the shallow bowl. Slice the cheese into ½ inch (1 cm) rounds and dust with flour, ensuring each slice is coated all over. Shake off any excess.

Dip the cheese into the egg, then fry in the hot oil for 1 minute on each side, or until crisp and golden. Drain on paper towels. Serve immediately, drizzled with honey and scattered with pine nuts.

SPICY *halloumi* BURGER

serves 2 / preparation : 6 minutes
equipment : large frying pan, small bowl, pastry brush

2 ciabatta rolls

9 oz (250 g) halloumi cheese

1 tablespoon harissa paste

2 ripe roma (plum) tomatoes

Heat 2 tablespoons olive oil in the frying pan. Meanwhile, mix the harissa paste with 1 tablespoon olive oil in the small bowl. Cut the tomatoes in half and slice the halloumi into 8 pieces.

Brush both sides of the halloumi with the harissa mixture and place in the frying pan. Add the tomatoes cut-side down. Fry for 1–2 minutes on each side, or until the halloumi is golden and starting to melt. Place 4 slices of halloumi and 2 tomato halves inside each roll. Serve with flat-leaf (Italian) parsley and mayonnaise on the side.

zucchini AND FETA FRITTERS

serves 4 / preparation : 10 minutes
equipment : large heavy frying pan, cheese grater, dish tea towel, bowl

1½ tablespoons all-purpose flour

A small handful of mint leaves

2 oz (50 g) feta cheese

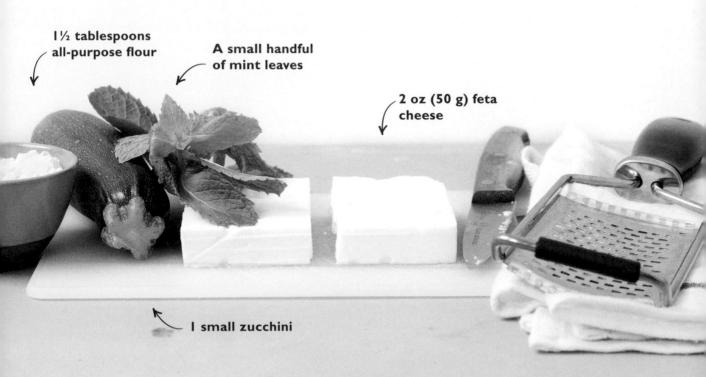

1 small zucchini

Set the frying pan over medium–high heat. Grate the zucchini, wrap in the dish towel, and squeeze to remove excess liquid. Finely chop the mint. In the bowl, combine the zucchini, mint, flour, and salt and pepper. Crumble in the feta, mix with your hands, and shape into 4 firm patties.

Add 2 tablespoons olive oil to the pan and fry the fritters for about 2 minutes on each side over medium–high heat, or until golden. Serve hot with leafy greens.

CHILI *eggplant*

serves 2 as a side / preparation : 10 minutes
equipment : gill pan, garlic press, small bowl, pastry brush

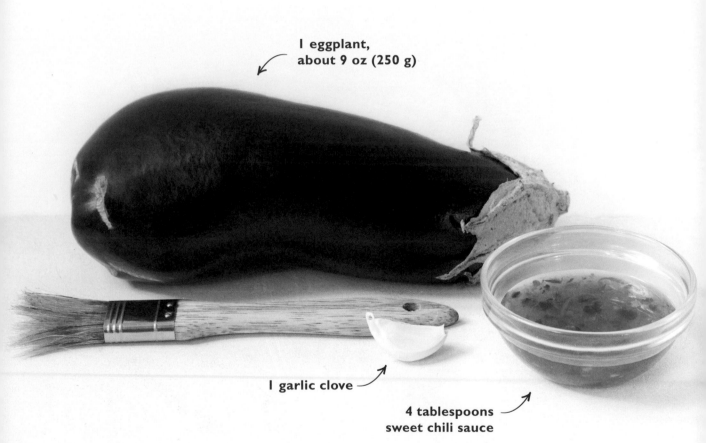

1 eggplant,
about 9 oz (250 g)

1 garlic clove

4 tablespoons
sweet chili sauce

Heat 2 tablespoons olive oil in the grill pan over high heat.
Meanwhile, crush the garlic into the small bowl and add the sweet chili
sauce, 1 tablespoon olive oil, and salt and pepper. Stir to combine.
Slice the eggplant into ⅛ inch (3 mm) slices. Brush on both sides with
the sweet chili sauce mixture. Cook for 1–2 minutes on each side on
the grill pan until they are tender and lightly charred.

leek AND GOAT CHEESE OMELET

serves 1 / preparation : 5 minutes
equipment : small non-stick frying pan, 2 small bowls, spatula

I small leek

2 oz (50 g) goat cheese

2 eggs

I tablespoon butter

Finely slice the leek, then gently fry in 2 tablespoons olive oil until tender, about 2 minutes. Season with salt and pepper, transfer to one of the bowls and set aside.

Wipe out the pan, add the butter, and place it over medium–high heat. Meanwhile, lightly beat the eggs in the other bowl, adding salt and pepper to taste. When the butter is foaming, add the eggs and cook undisturbed for 25 seconds. Use a spatula to push the eggs away from the edges of the pan to the center, tipping the pan to allow uncooked egg to fill the space. Continue until almost set, then place the leeks and crumbled goat cheese on one side. Fold the omelet in half. Cook for 30 seconds more, then slide onto a plate. Serve immediately with leafy greens.

tofu WITH SOUTH-EAST ASIAN DRESSING

serves 4 / preparation : 5 minutes
equipment : small bowl, small whisk or fork, grater

1 inch (3 cm) piece of fresh ginger

12 oz (350 g) block silken tofu

4 tablespoons soy sauce

1 tablespoon sugar

2 teaspoons dashi granules (or fish bouillon powder)

In the small bowl, whisk together the soy sauce, sugar, dashi granules, and 2 teaspoons cold water until the sugar dissolves.

Slice the tofu very thinly. Finely grate or chop the ginger. Serve the tofu sprinkled with the ginger and dressing.

asparagus AND PARMESAN TARTINE

serves 2 / preparation : 5 minutes
equipment : cheese grater, mixing bowl, vegetable peeler

A squeeze of lemon juice

6 asparagus spears

2 oz (50 g) parmesan cheese

2 slices of good quality rustic bread

Very finely grate the parmesan into the mixing bowl and add 2 tablespoons extra virgin olive oil and the lemon juice. Stir to make a paste.

Trim the asparagus and make ribbons using a vegetable peeler.

Spread the paste over the bread and top with the asparagus ribbons. Season with lots of black pepper.

tartine VARIATIONS

serves 2
For something different, try one of these variations
on the Asparagus and parmesan tartine
recipe on pages 56–57

4 tablespoons green olive tapenade

A handful of cornichons

4½ oz (130 g) frozen baby peas

2 teaspoons crème fraîche

A few slices of prosciutto

A squeeze of lemon juice

GREEN OLIVE TAPENADE AND PROSCIUTTO

Spread the green olive tapenade over 2 large slices of quality rustic bread. Top the tartine with wafer-thin slices of prosciutto and chopped cornichons.

PEA PURÉE AND MINT

Simmer the peas in water for 3 minutes. Drain. Add the crème fraîche, lemon, and a dash of olive oil. Mash. Season with salt and pepper and spread over 2 slices of good quality rustic bread. Scatter with chopped fresh mint.

1 small red onion

1 apple

1 tablespoon
capers

3 tablespoons
crème fraîche

2 teaspoons
honey

2 tablespoons
ricotta

7 oz (200 g) can
tuna in oil

1½ tablespoons
Dijon mustard

TUNA RILLETTES

Place the tuna in a bowl with the red onion (grated), the capers (finely chopped), the mustard, the crème fraîche, and 2 tablespoons extra virgin olive oil. Mash thoroughly with a fork and season with salt and pepper. Spread onto 2 slices of good quality rustic bread.

RICOTTA, APPLE, AND HONEY

Spread 2 slices of quality rustic bread with the ricotta. Peel and core the apple, slice it thinly, and arrange on top of the ricotta. Drizzle with honey.

tartine VARIATIONS

serves 2
For something different, try one of these variations
on the Asparagus and parmesan tartine
recipe on pages 56–57

A handful of radishes

4½ oz (125 g) soft goat cheese

Mixed seeds, for sprinkling

½ tablespoon lemon juice

3½ oz (100 g/ ½ cup) hummus

A squeeze of lemon

1 garlic clove

1 tablespoon chives

Cilantro leaves, to finish

2 teaspoons finely grated lemon zest

GOAT CHEESE, CHIVES, RADISH

Mash together the goat cheese, lemon, the chives (snipped), the garlic (crushed), and black pepper. Spread over 2 large slices of quality rustic bread and top with very finely sliced radishes and a sprinkling of sea salt.

LEMON HUMMUS WITH MIXED SEEDS AND CILANTRO

Mix the hummus with the lemon juice and zest. Spread over 2 large slices of quality rustic bread, sprinkle with mixed seeds, and top with cilantro leaves.

4½ oz (125 g) can cannellini beans (drained weight)

4 tablespoons Greek-style yogurt

A couple slices of smoked salmon

A spritz of lemon juice

A handful of caper berries

1 tablespoon chopped dill

1 garlic clove

A few slices of chorizo

1 tablespoon fromage blanc or 1 tablespoon each of olive oil and Greek-style yogurt

GARLICKY BEAN PURÉE AND CHORIZO

Blend the cannellini beans, garlic, yogurt, and 1 tablespoon olive oil in a blender until creamy. Season generously with salt and pepper. Spread over 2–4 slices of quality rustic bread and top with sliced chorizo.

FROMAGE BLANC, SMOKED SALMON, AND DILL

Mix together the fromage blanc (or oil and yogurt), and chopped dill. Spread over 2 large slices of quality rustic bread. Arrange the smoked salmon (finely sliced) on top, and finish with caper berries and a spritz of lemon.

CHAPTER 2

salads & soups

lemony
shaved salad

serves 2 as a starter / preparation : 10 minutes
equipment : mandoline, vegetable peeler

Trim the fennel and radishes and slice very thinly on the mandoline. Create long shavings of asparagus by drawing the peeler from the woody end to the tip of the stalk.

Whisk the lemon juice with 1 tablespoon extra virgin olive oil. Season with salt and pepper. Arrange the vegetables on serving plates and finish by drizzling with the dressing.

6–8 asparagus spears

3 oz (80 g) radishes

1 fennel bulb

1 tablespoon lemon juice

beet AND GOAT CHEESE SALAD

serves 2 as a starter or side / preparation : 5 minutes
equipment : whisk, small bowl

4 tablespoons soft goat cheese

4 small cooked beets

I tablespoon lemon juice

2–3 sprigs of thyme

Whisk together the lemon juice, 2 tablespoons extra virgin olive oil, most of the leaves from the thyme sprigs, and salt and pepper.

Cut each beet in half, and then each half in half again. Pour most of the dressing over the beets and toss to coat. Spoon goat cheese over the top, and then drizzle with the rest of the dressing. Season generously and sprinkle with the rest of the thyme leaves.

broccolini SALAD

serves 4 as a side / preparation : 10 minutes
equipment : saucepan, bowl of iced water, small and a large bowl

2 tablespoons
rice vinegar

1½ tablespoon
lime juice

A pinch of dashi
granules or fish
bouillon powder

10½ oz (300 g)
broccolini (or
broccoli)

1 tablespoon soy sauce

Fill the saucepan with water and bring it to a boil. Meanwhile, cut the broccolini into small florets. Generously season the boiling water with salt, and blanch the broccolini for about 2 minutes. It should still be slightly crisp. Drain and plunge in the iced water.

In the small bowl, whisk together the soy sauce, rice vinegar, lime juice, and dashi granules, plus a splash of cold water. Drain the broccolini, transfer it to the large bowl, and toss with enough of the dressing to coat. Add salt and pepper to taste.

WARM RADICCHIO AND
grain SALAD

serves 2 / preparation: 10 minutes
equipment : 2 small bowls, large frying pan

9 oz (250 g)
ready-to-eat
grains, such as
quinoa, farro,
or a mixture

1 tablespoon
lemon juice,
plus extra
for serving

5½ oz (150 g)
radicchio

2 oz (60 g/⅓ cup)
dried cranberries,
cherries, or
golden raisins

½ teaspoon Dijon
mustard

Boil water in a large pot. Meanwhile, slice the radicchio. In one of the bowls, whisk together the lemon juice, the mustard, 2 tablespoons extra virgin olive oil, and salt and pepper.

Place the dried fruit in the other bowl and cover with boiling water. Set aside. Heat 2 tablespoons olive oil in the frying pan and add the grains and the radicchio. Gently stir-fry until the grains are warmed through and the radicchio is just tender. Remove from the heat. Drain the dried fruit and add to the frying pan. Stir through the dressing. Season with sea salt flakes and pour over extra lemon juice before serving.

lardon SALAD

serves 2 / preparation: 6 minutes
equipment : small frying pan, salad bowl

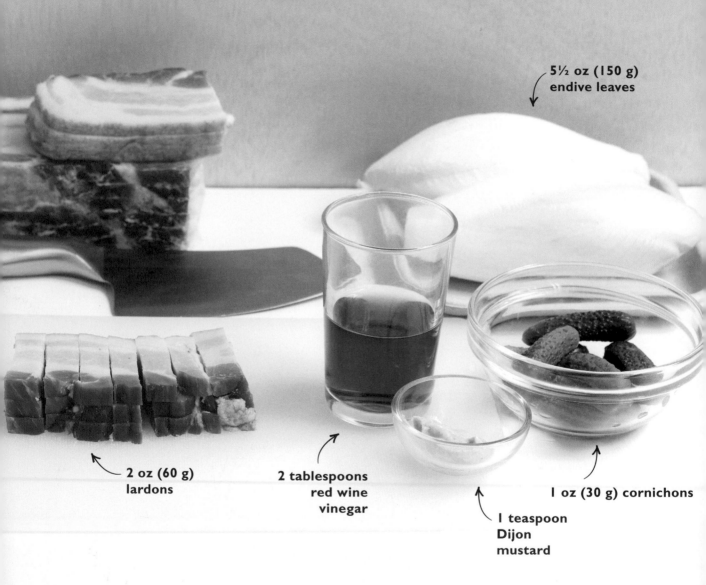

**5½ oz (150 g)
endive leaves**

**2 oz (60 g)
lardons**

**2 tablespoons
red wine
vinegar**

**1 teaspoon
Dijon
mustard**

1 oz (30 g) cornichons

Roughly chop the cornichons. Set the frying pan over high heat.

Pour 3 tablespoons extra virgin olive oil into the salad bowl, add the mustard and salt and pepper, and whisk. Add the cornichons and endive leaves, but don't toss.

Fry the lardons in a splash of olive oil for about 3 minutes, until crisp. Add the vinegar, stir, and let the liquid bubble for about 30 seconds. Pour the lardons and pan juices over the salad and toss well.

73

SIMPLE *fatoush*

serves 2 / preparation : 8 minutes
equipment : salad bowl

I small
cucumber

2 ripe tomatoes

I tablespoon
lemon juice

I piece flatbread
or I flour tortilla

I teaspoon
ground sumac

Heat the flatbread until crisp and golden. Meanwhile, in the salad bowl, whisk together the lemon juice, 1 tablespoon extra virgin olive oil, and salt and pepper.

Dice the tomatoes and cucumbers and break up the bread into bite-sized pieces. Add to the salad bowl, sprinkle with ground sumac, taste for seasoning. and gently toss.

FIG AND *spinach* SALAD

serves 2 / preparation: 5 minutes
equipment : salad bowl

2 oz (60 g/
1½ cups) baby
spinach leaves

1½ teaspoons
harissa paste

1 tablespoon
lemon juice

4 fresh figs

In the salad bowl, whisk together the harissa paste, lemon juice, 1½ tablespoons extra virgin olive oil, and 1 tablespoon cold water. Add salt and pepper to taste.

Cut the figs into quarters lengthways and add to the bowl, along with the baby spinach. Gently toss, ensuring that the spinach leaves are coated in dressing.

herb SALAD

serves 2 as a starter or side / preparation : 3 minutes
equipment : salad bowl

**A few chopped
walnuts, for sprinkling**

**A squeeze
of lemon
juice**

**I oz (30 g) mixed herbs
or microgreens such as
flat-leaf parsley, mint,
basil, red amaranth,
arugula, pea shoots,
cilantro and radish tops**

**Walnut oil, for
drizzling**

Combine the mixed herbs (or microgreens) and walnuts in the bowl. Squeeze the lemon over the top and drizzle with walnut oil. Season with salt and pepper and lightly toss before serving.

tomato, MOZZARELLA, AND BASIL SALAD

serves 2 as a main (or 4 as a starter)
preparation : 3 minutes
equipment : large serving plate

3 ripe heirloom tomatoes

2 balls of buffalo mozzarella

10 basil leaves

Thinly slice the tomatoes and slice the mozzarella. Arrange on the plate. Season with sea salt flakes and freshly ground black pepper, and scatter with the basil leaves. Drizzle with some extra virgin olive oil before serving.

tomato, MOZZARELLA, AND BASIL VARIATIONS

serves 2 as a main (or 4 as a starter)
For something different, try one of these variations
on the Tomato, mozzarella, and basil salad on pages 80–81

**3 tablespoons
extra virgin
olive oil**

**1 tablespoon
balsamic
vinegar**

4 figs

**6 slices
of prosciutto**

**9 thin
asparagus
spears**

FIGS AND PROSCIUTTO

Arrange the figs (halved lengthways), the slices of prosciutto, 2 mozzarella balls (sliced), and 10 basil leaves on a plate. Whisk together the extra virgin olive oil and the balsamic vinegar and drizzle over the salad.

ASPARAGUS

Heat a grill pan, while you prepare the tomatoes and mozzarella, as instructed on pages 80–81. Toss the asparagus spears in olive oil and grill for 4–6 minutes, turning regularly, until tender and charred. Add to the plate with the tomatoes and mozzarella and drizzle with extra virgin olive oil.

1 tablespoon capers

3 anchovy fillets in oil

1 ripe avocado

A handful of pea shoots

½ garlic clove

ANCHOVIES AND CAPERS

Prepare the tomato, mozzarella, and basil salad on pages 80–81, but omit the basil. Mix together the anchovies (chopped), garlic (crushed), capers (chopped), and 4 tablespoons olive oil. Drizzle over the salad.

AVOCADO AND PEA SHOOTS

Prepare the tomato, mozzarella, and basil salad on pages 80–81, but add the ripe avocado (sliced) to the serving plate, and scatter with pea shoots instead of basil.

vegetable REMOULADE

serves 2 as a starter / preparation : 10 minutes
equipment : mandoline or food processor with julienne blade or
a grater, bowl

2 big carrots

2 tablespoons crème fraîche

7 oz (200 g) raw beets

3 teaspoons za'tar

2 tablespoons mayonnaise

Peel and shred the beets and carrots using the mandoline or food processor. Add to the bowl with the mayonnaise, crème fraîche, and za'tar, and gently fold in the vegetables. Season generously with salt and freshly ground black pepper. Serve immediately or chill, until ready, to let the flavors develop.

chickpea SALAD

serves 2 as a starter / preparation : 5 minutes
equipment : salad bowl, colander

I red onion

I small handful of parsley

14 oz (400 g) can of chickpeas

½–I teaspoon ground cumin

I tablespoon lemon juice

Finely chop the red onion, place in the salad bowl with the lemon juice and a generous pinch of sea salt flakes. Mix and set aside. Roughly chop the parsley leaves and add to the bowl.

Drain and rinse the chickpeas, shaking off as much water as possible. Add to the bowl along with the cumin (to taste), freshly ground black pepper, and 1 tablespoon extra virgin olive oil. Toss to combine and taste for seasoning, adding more salt, pepper, or lemon juice to taste.

SPRING *couscous*

serves 4 as a side / preparation : 10 minutes
equipment : large heatproof bowl

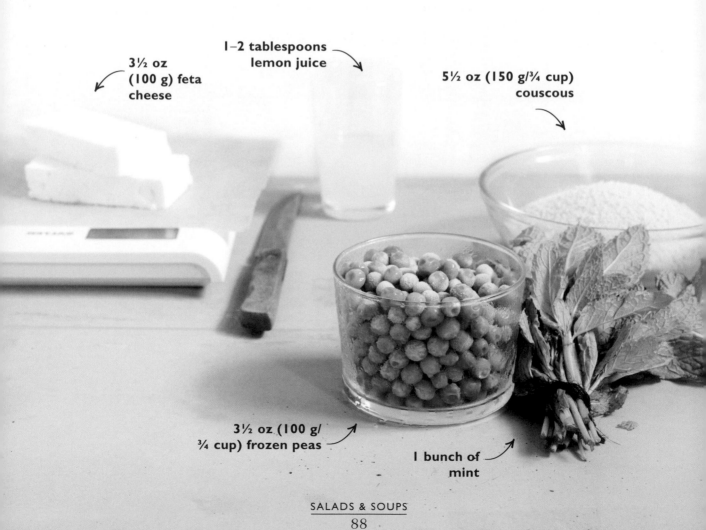

3½ oz (100 g) feta cheese

1–2 tablespoons lemon juice

5½ oz (150 g/¾ cup) couscous

3½ oz (100 g/ ¾ cup) frozen peas

1 bunch of mint

Boil 17 fl oz (500 ml/2 cups) water in a small pan. Meanwhile, roughly chop the mint and cut the feta into bite-size pieces. Put the couscous in the bowl with the boiling water, the peas, and a generous pinch of sea salt. Mix, cover with plastic wrap, and set aside for 5 minutes.

Add the mint, 1 tablespoon extra virgin olive oil, 1 tablespoon of the lemon juice, and salt and pepper to the couscous. Use a fork to combine thoroughly. Taste for seasoning and add more lemon juice or salt and pepper, if needed. Scatter with the feta and serve.

GRILLED *Little Gems*
WITH DUKKAH

serves 2 as a starter / preparation : 10 minutes
*equipment : grill pan or heavy frying pan, garlic press, pastry brush,
serving plate*

2½ oz (75 g) cherry tomatoes

2 Little Gem lettuces

2 tablespoons dukkah

1 garlic clove

1 tablespoon lemon juice

Set the grill pan or frying pan over high heat. Meanwhile, crush the garlic and whisk it together with 3 tablespoons extra virgin olive oil, the lemon juice, and salt and pepper. Set aside.

Cut the lettuces in half lengthways, brush the cut side with the garlicky dressing and sear cut-side down for 2 minutes. Turn over and repeat. Place the lettuces on the serving plate. Halve the tomatoes and scatter them over the lettuce leaves. Drizzle with some of the remaining dressing and serve, sprinkled with the dukkah.

burrata WITH GRILLED PEACHES

serves 4 / preparation : 10 minutes
equipment : baking sheet lined with foil, serving plate

4 ripe peaches

A handful of arugula leaves

2 x 7 oz (200 g) balls of burrata

1 tablespoon balsamic vinegar

Place a grill pan on the stove over high heat. Halve and pit the peaches. Cut each half into 2 slices and place on the baking sheet. Grill for 2 minutes on each side, or until the peaches start to char.

Whisk together 3 tablespoons extra virgin olive oil, the balsamic vinegar, and salt and pepper. Slice or break open the burrata and arrange on a serving plate with the grilled peaches. Scatter with the arugula and drizzle with the dressing. Serve immediately.

burrata VARIATIONS

serves 2
For something different, try one of these variations
on the Burrata with grilled peaches
recipe on pages 92–93

2 tablespoons
orange juice

3½ oz (100 g)
asparagus tips

2 tablespoons
butter

2 garlic cloves

1½ tablespoons
coriander seeds

2 tablespoons
chopped cilantro

ORANGE AND CILANTRO

Lightly toast the coriander seeds in a hot pan for about 2 minutes. Lightly crush with a mortar and pestle. Whisk together the chopped cilantro, orange juice, and 2 tablespoons olive oil. Stir in the coriander seeds. Slice or tear open 2 x 7 oz (200 g) balls of burrata and spoon over the dressing.

ASPARAGUS AND GARLIC BUTTER

Heat I tablespoon olive oil in a frying pan and sauté the asparagus over high heat for 2–3 minutes until bright green. Turn the heat to low, add the garlic (thinly sliced) and butter, and cook for I minute. Slice or tear open 2 x 7 oz (200 g) burrata and serve with asparagus and the butter poured over.

FAVA BEANS AND MINT

Cook the beans in salted boiling water for about 4 minutes until tender. Meanwhile, whisk together 3 tablespoons extra virgin olive oil, the lemon juice, the mint leaves (finely chopped), salt, and pepper.

Drain the beans, rinse under cold water, and toss with the dressing. Slice or tear open 2 x 7 oz (200 g) balls of burrata and spoon the beans and dressing over the top.

3½ oz (100 g/ ½ cup) frozen fava beans

1 tablespoon lemon juice

2 teaspoons finely grated lemon zest

1 oz (30 g/½ cup) breadcrumbs

2 teaspoons chopped oregano leaves

10 mint leaves

2 garlic cloves

OREGANO PANGRATTATO

Heat 1 tablespoon olive oil in a frying pan and toast the breadcrumbs and the garlic cloves (crushed) over medium heat for about 2 minutes, until golden.

Remove to a bowl and stir through the oregano and lemon zest. Slice or tear open 2 x 7 oz (200 g) balls of burrata, sprinkle with the breadcrumbs, and drizzle with extra virgin olive oil.

ROASTED *red pepper* SOUP

serves 2 / preparation : 10 minutes
equipment : large heavy pan, blender

9 oz (250 g) drained roasted red peppers from a jar, plus 2 tablespoons jar oil

1 onion

5 basil leaves

2 garlic cloves

Enough vegetable bouillon cubes or bouillon powder to make 14 fl oz (400 ml/ 1½ cups) stock

Boil 14 fl oz (400 ml/1½ cups) water in a small pot. Roughly chop the onion and garlic. Heat the 2 tablespoons oil, from the jar of red peppers, in the large heavy pan and gently fry the onion and garlic for 5 minutes. Meanwhile, roughly chop the peppers and add them to the pan. Stir.

Pour the boiling water into the pan and add the bouillon cube or bouillon powder. Stir. Season with salt and pepper.

Transfer to the blender, add the basil, and blend to the desired consistency. Add a little more boiling water or salt and pepper, if needed. Serve hot or chilled with bread and butter.

CHILI *beef* BROTH

serves 2 / preparation : 10 minutes
equipment : grill pan, saucepan

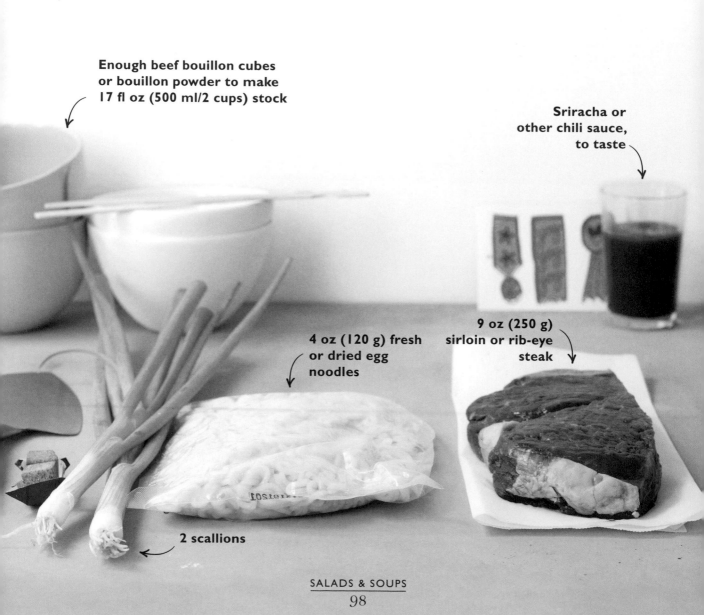

Enough beef bouillon cubes or bouillon powder to make 17 fl oz (500 ml/2 cups) stock

Sriracha or other chili sauce, to taste

4 oz (120 g) fresh or dried egg noodles

9 oz (250 g) sirloin or rib-eye steak

2 scallions

Boil 17 fl oz (500 ml/2 cups) water in the saucepan. Set the grill pan over high heat. Meanwhile, finely slice the scallions. Rub the steak with a little vegetable oil and generously season with salt and freshly ground black pepper.

Add the bouillon cubes or powder, scallions, noodles, and Sriracha sauce to the boiling water in the saucepan. Stir and simmer gently.

Cook the steak on the grill pan for 3–4 minutes, or to your liking, turning every 30 seconds or so. Wrap loosely in foil and set aside to rest.

Pour the soup and noodles into bowls. Slice the steak and add to the bowls.

miso SOUP WITH TOFU

serves 2 / preparation : 6 minutes
equipment : saucepan, small bowl

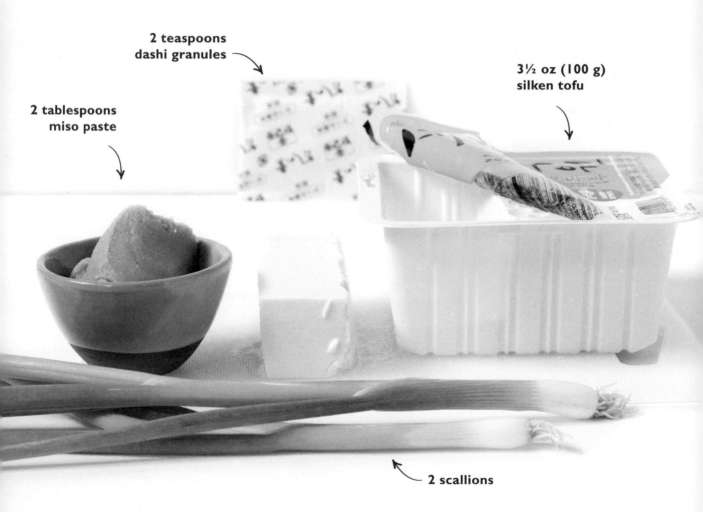

2 teaspoons
dashi granules

3½ oz (100 g)
silken tofu

2 tablespoons
miso paste

2 scallions

Boil 17 fl oz (500 ml/2 cups) water in the saucepan. Meanwhile, finely slice the scallions and cut the tofu into ½ inch (1 cm) dice.

Add the dashi granules to the boiling water in the pan. Stir over medium heat until completely dissolved. Add the scallions and tofu and gently simmer for 1 minute to warm through the tofu.

Place the miso paste in a small bowl, add 2 tablespoons of the dashi broth, and whisk. Pour into the pan and stir well. Serve the miso soup immediately.

pea AND HAM SOUP

serves 4 / preparation : 6 minutes
equipment : large saucepan, blender

14 oz (400 g/ 3 cups) frozen baby peas

3 teaspoons crème fraîche

3½ oz (100 g) ham

Enough chicken bouillon cubes or powder to make 21 fl oz (600 ml/ 2½ cups) stock

Boil 21 fl oz (600 ml/2½ cups) water in the saucepan and add the bouillon cubes or bouillon powder, the peas, and mint. Simmer for 4 minutes. Meanwhile, dice the ham.

Pour the peas and the stock into the blender and add half the ham. Blend until smooth. Add more water, if too thick.

Return to the pan, add the crème fraîche, and warm through, stirring. Season with salt and pepper. Serve sprinkled with the remaining ham.

chili SOUP

serves 2 / preparation : 5 minutes
equipment : blender, saucepan

1 x 14 oz (400 g) can red kidney beans

7 oz (200 g) chopped canned tomatoes

½ teaspoon ground cumin

2 teaspoons chipotle paste or 1 teaspoon smoked paprika

Enough beef bouillon cubes or bouillon powder to make 7 fl oz (200 ml/¾ cup) stock

Boil 7 fl oz (200 ml/¾ cup) water in a small pan. Place all the ingredients in the blender with the boiling water and blend until smooth. Pour the soup into the pan and set over medium heat to warm through.

cauliflower
MASALA SOUP

serves 4 / preparation : 10 minutes
equipment : cheese grater, 2 large saucepans, blender

Enough vegetable bouillon
cubes or bouillon powder to
make 35 fl oz (1 litre/
4 cups) stock

1 lb (450 g)
cauliflower

3 tablespoons
heavy cream

1 tablespoon
garam masala

Boil 35 fl oz (1 litre/4 cups) water in a large saucepan. Meanwhile, grate the cauliflower. Heat 2 tablespoons olive oil in another saucepan, add the cauliflower and garam masala, and cook, stirring, over medium heat for a few minutes, until the cauliflower softens but doesn't color.

Pour the boiling water into the cauliflower mixture, add the bouillon cubes or bouillon powder, and stir. Simmer for 5 minutes.

Transfer the mixture to a blender and process until smooth. Return to the pan, add the cream and salt and pepper to taste, and cook over gentle heat until warmed through. Serve with bread.

white bean SOUP

serves 2 / preparation : 5 minutes
equipment : blender, saucepan

2 tablespoons tahini

2 x 14 oz (400 g) cans cannellini beans

2 garlic cloves

Enough vegetable bouillon cubes or bouillon powder to make 14 fl oz (400 ml/ 1½ cups) stock

1 teaspoon ras el hanout

Boil 14 fl oz (400 ml/1½ cups) water in a small pan.

Drain the beans, reserving 2 tablespoons of the liquid from the can.

Blend the beans in the blender with 10½ fl oz (300 ml/1¼ cups) of the boiling water, the stock, garlic, tahini, ras el hanout, 2 tablespoons extra virgin olive oil, and the reserved liquid from the can. Generously season with salt and pepper. Add more boiling water, if too thick.

Pour the soup into the saucepan and warm through over medium heat. Taste for seasoning and serve immediately.

CREAMY *avocado* SOUP

serves 2 as a main (or 4 as a starter)
preparation : 5 minutes
equipment : blender

Tabasco®, to taste

5½ oz (150 g/ ¾ cup) corn kernels from a can

2½ fl oz (75 ml/ ⅓ cup) lime juice

8 fl oz (240 ml/1 cup) coconut milk

2 ripe avocados

Scoop out the avocado flesh and place in the blender with the corn kernels, coconut milk, lime juice, Tabasco, 13 fl oz (380 ml/1½ cups) cold water, and lots of salt and pepper. Blend until smooth. Add more water, if too thick, and taste for seasoning.

Serve with ice cubes or chill in the fridge, if you have time.

tomato AND BREAD SOUP

serves 2 or 4 / preparation : 10 minutes
equipment : medium and a large bowl, blender, sieve

3 tablespoons blanched slivered almonds

3 oz (80 g) stale white bread

2 garlic cloves

Serrano ham, to serve

2 lb 4oz (1 kg) ripe tomatoes

Tear the bread into pieces, place in the medium bowl, and pour in a little cold water. Set aside. Roughly chop the tomatoes and garlic and place in the food processor or blender with the almonds. Blend until as smooth as possible.

Strain through the sieve into the large bowl, pressing down with the back of a spoon, then discard the solids and return the rest of the mixture to the blender. Add the soaked bread and 1½ tablespoons extra virgin olive oil, ½ teaspoon sea salt flakes, and blend until smooth. Add a little water, if too thick. Chill before serving, if you have time.

Finely chop the ham and sprinkle over the soup before serving.

MINTY *cucumber* SOUP

serves 2 / preparation : 8 minutes
equipment : frying pan, blender, 5 ice cubes, plus more for serving

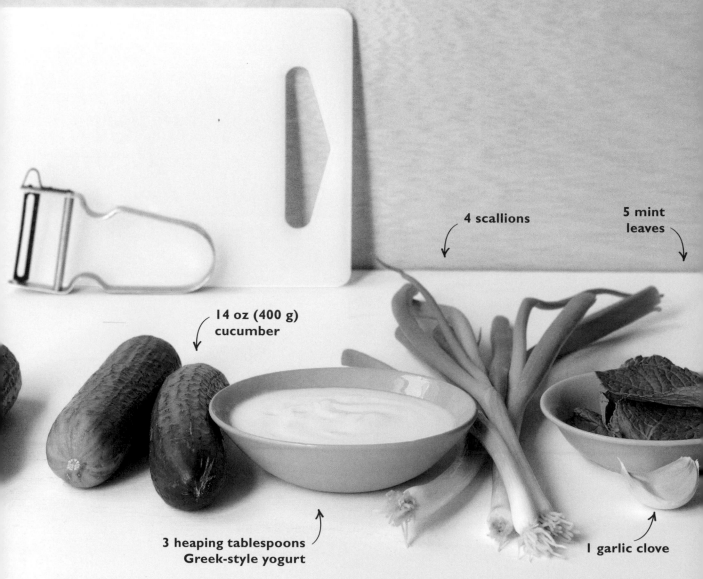

4 scallions

5 mint leaves

14 oz (400 g) cucumber

3 heaping tablespoons Greek-style yogurt

1 garlic clove

Peel and roughly chop the cucumber. Slice the scallions and the garlic. Gently fry the cucumber, scallions, and garlic in 1–2 tablespoons olive oil for about 2 minutes, until soft. Season with sea salt flakes and freshly ground black pepper.

Transfer to the blender, add the mint and the 5 ice cubes and blend until smooth, or the desired consistency. Add the yogurt and blend again. Serve with ice cubes.

BASIC *vegetable* SOUP

serves 4 / preparation : 10 minutes
equipment : 2 large saucepans, garlic press

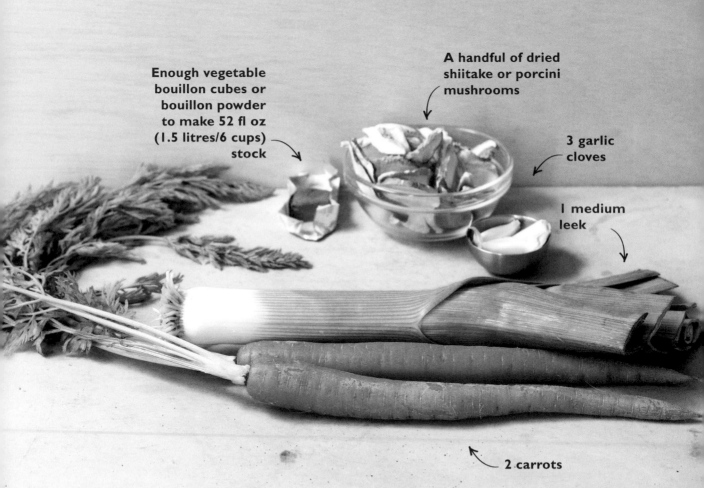

Enough vegetable
bouillon cubes or
bouillon powder
to make 52 fl oz
(1.5 litres/6 cups)
stock

A handful of dried
shiitake or porcini
mushrooms

3 garlic
cloves

1 medium
leek

2 carrots

Fill a saucepan with 52 fl oz (1.5 litres/6 cups) water and bring it to a boil. Heat 2 tablespoons olive oil in another large saucepan over medium heat. Peel and cut the carrots into small dice, then add to the pan and stir. Finely slice the leek, then add to the pan and stir. Crush the garlic, then add to the pan and stir. Cook for 2 more minutes.

Pour the boiling water into the pan, then add the bouillon cubes or bouillon powder and the mushrooms. Stir. Simmer for 5 minutes. Taste for seasoning.

VEGETABLE *soup* VARIATIONS

serves 4
For something different, try one of these variations on the Basic vegetable soup recipe on pages 116–117

5½ oz (150 g) rice noodles

1½ teaspoons harissa paste

SPICY

Stir in the harissa paste when adding the stock.

NOODLES

Add the rice noodles, when adding the stock, and cook the soup until warmed through.

14 oz (400 g) can drained beans such as black, cannellini, borlotti, or kidney beans

2 tablespoons toasted pine nuts

2 tablespoons finely chopped parsely

Finely grated zest of 1 lemon

PINE NUT GREMOLATA

Mix together the chopped parsley, the lemon zest, and the toasted pine nuts (chopped). Sprinkle over the soup to serve.

BEANS

Add the beans to the soup with the mushrooms. Taste for seasoning, as beans need lots of salt and pepper.

CHAPTER 3

pasta

BASIC *tomato sauce*

serves 4 / preparation : 10 minutes
equipment : heavy frying pan, large saucepan, slotted spoon

14 oz (400 g) fresh
penne

1 lb 2oz (500 g/2 cups)
puréed tomatoes

2 garlic cloves

A handful of
basil leaves

Fill a saucepan with water and bring it to a boil. Heat the frying pan. Meanwhile, peel and bruise the garlic with the flat side of a knife. Add the pasta to the boiling water. Cook according to the instructions on the package. Drain, toss with olive oil, and set aside.

Meanwhile, add 2 tablespoons olive oil to the frying pan and then the garlic. Cook, stirring, over medium heat, until the garlic starts to color. Remove the garlic with a slotted spoon and discard. Add the puréed tomatoes and simmer until reduced a little, stirring frequently. Generously season with sea salt flakes and pepper. Tear the basil leaves and add to the sauce. Stir through the drained pasta and serve.

tomato sauce
VARIATIONS

serves 4

For something different, try one of these variations on the Basic tomato sauce recipe on pages 122–123

4 anchovy fillets in oil

1½ oz (40 g/⅓ cup) black olives

4 eggs

1–2 teaspoons chipotle, sriracha, or other chili sauce

¼ teaspoon chili flakes (or more to taste)

RANCHOS HUEVOS

Make the basic tomato recipe, but leave out the basil. Stir in the chili sauce. Crack the eggs into the pan and cook for 2 minutes over medium heat. Cover, reduce the heat, and cook for 1–2 minutes until the whites of the eggs are set, but the yolks still runny.

CHILI FLAKES, OLIVES, AND ANCHOVIES

Make the basic tomato sauce recipe, adding the anchovy fillets (chopped) with the garlic. Add the black olives (chopped) and the chili flakes to the puréed tomatoes. Simmer for a few minutes before serving with pasta.

2 zucchini

1 red bell pepper

3½ oz (100 g) smoked bacon or chorizo

1 tablespoon chopped thyme

2 garlic cloves

SIMPLE RATATOUILLE

Thinly slice the zucchini, bell pepper, and garlic. Fry in 2 tablespoons olive oil until tender. Add 1 lb 2oz (500 g/ 2 cups) puréed tomatoes and continue to follow the basic tomato sauce recipe, but do not remove the garlic. Serve as a pasta sauce or to accompany fish or chicken.

WITH BACON OR CHORIZO

Chop the bacon or chorizo, and fry in a splash of olive oil, until crisp at the edges. Add the garlic and cook for 1 minute. Add 1 lb 2 oz (500 g/ 2 cups) puréed tomatoes, the chopped thyme, salt, and pepper. Simmer for a few minutes before serving with pasta.

SPAGHETTI *carbonara*

serves 2 / preparation : 10 minutes
equipment : cheese grater, mixing bowl, large saucepan, frying pan

9 oz (250 g) fresh spaghetti

3 oz (100 g) smoked lardons

2 eggs, plus 1 egg yolk

2 oz (50 g) parmesan cheese, plus extra for sprinkling

Bring a large saucepan of water to a boil. Meanwhile, grate the parmesan into the bowl and add the eggs and yolk. Mix well and season with some pepper.

Generously season the boiling water with fine sea salt, and add the spaghetti. Cook according to the instructions on the package. Drain, reserving a few tablespoonfuls of the cooking water, toss with olive oil, and set aside.

Meanwhile, in the frying pan, fry the lardons in 1 tablespoon olive oil until crisp at the edges. Add the pasta, a little of the reserved pasta water, and toss to coat. Add the egg mixture and stir over very low heat, until the egg and liquid reduces to a creamy sauce. Serve immediately, sprinkled with the extra parmesan.

avocado PESTO GNOCCHI

serves 2 generously / preparation : 6 minutes
equipment : food processor or blender, large saucepan

I ripe avocado

1 oz (35 g/ ¼ cup) pine nuts

A handful of basil leaves

14 oz (400 g) gnocchi

I–2 garlic cloves

Bring a large saucepan of water to a boil. Peel the garlic cloves and place in the food processor or blender. Scoop in the avocado flesh and add the pine nuts, basil, 1½ tablespoons extra virgin olive oil, and some salt and black pepper. Blend until smooth.

Generously season the boiling water with fine sea salt, and add the gnocchi. Cook according to the instructions on the package, then drain. Stir through the avocado pesto and drizzle with extra virgin olive oil. Serve immediately.

lemon AND RICOTTA LINGUINE

serves 2 / preparation : 5 minutes
equipment : cheese grater, large saucepan, frying pan, colander

9 oz (250 g) fresh linguine

1 lemon

5½ oz (150 g) ricotta cheese

1 garlic clove

A small handful of basil leaves

Bring a large saucepan of water to a boil. Meanwhile, thinly slice the garlic and finely grate the lemon zest. Generously season the boiling water with fine sea salt, and cook the pasta according to the instructions on the package. Drain, reserving some of the cooking water, toss with olive oil, and set aside.

Meanwhile, stir together the lemon zest, the ricotta, and a squeeze of lemon until creamy. Gently fry the garlic in 1 tablespoon olive oil until it turns pale gold. Remove from the heat. Add the pasta and gently toss. Add the ricotta mixture and the pasta cooking water, and stir over medium–low heat, until the sauce is reduced and creamy. Season well with salt and pepper. Scatter over torn basil leaves and serve immediately.

PASTA WITH *sardines*, PINE NUTS, AND RAISINS

serves 2 / preparation : 10 minutes
equipment : garlic press, frying pan, large saucepan, colander

1 lb 2oz (500 g) fresh spaghetti

2 tablespoons raisins

2 garlic cloves

2 tablespoons pine nuts

5½ oz (150 g) canned sardines (drained weight)

Bring a large saucepan of water to a boil. Meanwhile, crush the garlic and set the frying pan over medium–high heat. Generously season the boiling water with fine sea salt, and cook the pasta according to the instructions on the package. Drain, reserving a few tablespoons of the cooking water, and toss with olive oil.

Meanwhile, heat 2 tablespoons of oil from the sardine cans in the frying pan and gently cook the garlic until aromatic. Add the sardines, breaking them up with a spoon. Reduce the heat to low and add the pine nuts and raisins, stirring to warm through. Add the pasta to the frying pan and gently toss, adding some of the reserved cooking water to loosen. Serve immediately.

clam AND TARRAGON PASTA

serves 4 / preparation : 10 minutes
equipment : 2 large saucepans (1 with a lid)

9 fl oz (250 ml/1 cup)
dry white wine

1 lb 2 oz (500 g)
fresh spaghetti

2 lb 4 oz (1 kg)
small clams
(shell on)

3 garlic cloves

2 tarragon leaves

Bring a large saucepan of water to a boil. Meanwhile, finely chop the garlic and chop the tarragon. Generously season the boiling water with fine sea salt, and cook the spaghetti according to the instructions on the package. Drain, drizzle with olive oil, and set aside.

Meanwhile, heat 3 tablespoons olive oil in the lidded saucepan and gently cook the garlic until aromatic. Add the clams (discarding any unopened ones) and white wine. Cover and cook for about 4 minutes, shaking the pan frequently, until almost all the clams have opened. Discard any unopened ones. Add the pasta, tarragon, and salt and pepper. Gently toss. Serve immediately with all the pan juices.

ORZO AND *cavolo nero* STEW

serves 4 / preparation : 10 minutes
equipment : 2 large heavy saucepans

7 oz (200 g) tomatoes

Enough vegetable bouillon cubes or bouillon powder to make 26 fl oz (750 ml/ 3 cups) stock

7 oz (200 g) orzo

2½ oz (75 g) cavolo nero (black kale)

1 tablespoon tomato paste (concentrated purée)

Boil 35 fl oz (1 litre/4 cups) water in a large saucepan. Meanwhile, slice the kale, discarding any tough stalks. Roughly chop the tomatoes.

Pour 26 fl oz (750 ml/3 cups) boiling water into another saucepan and add the stock, orzo, kale, tomatoes, and tomato paste. Generously season with salt and pepper. Gently boil for 7–8 minutes, stirring frequently to prevent sticking, until the orzo is tender. Add more boiling water, if too thick. Taste for seasoning before serving.

FETTUCINE WITH WHITE SAUCE *(alfredo)*

serves 2 / preparation : 6 minutes
equipment : large and a medium saucepan, grater

**7 fl oz (200 ml)
heavy cream**

**3 tablespoons
butter**

**3 oz (80 g)
parmesan
cheese**

**9 oz (250 g) fresh
fettucine**

Bring a large saucepan of water to a boil. Add the fettuccini, and season generously with fine sea salt. Cook according to the instructions on the package. Drain and toss with olive oil. Set aside.

Meanwhile, melt the butter and cream together in the medium pan over medium–low heat. Stir, then remove from the heat. Grate the parmesan and add to the cream mixture. Return to low heat and stir until melted. Season with salt and pepper. Stir the white sauce through the pasta and serve immediately.

WHITE SAUCE *(alfredo)* VARIATIONS

serves 2
For something different, try one of these variations on the Fettucine with
white sauce (alfredo) recipe on pages 138–139

7 oz (200 g) mushrooms

2 oz (60 g/ ½ cup) frozen peas

2½ oz (75 g) lardons

4 tablespoons butter

2 garlic cloves

MUSHROOMS

Make the basic cream sauce, then finely slice the mushrooms and crush the garlic. Sauté the mushrooms and garlic in the butter for **3 minutes**, or until the mushrooms are tender. Season and add to the cream sauce.

BACON AND PEAS

Make the basic cream sauce, then add the frozen peas. Cook, stirring, over low heat until the peas are tender. Set aside. Fry the lardons until crisp and add to the sauce.

10½ oz (300 g) smoked salmon

3 oz (80 g/ 2 cups) baby spinach leaves

1 tablespoon chopped dill

SMOKED SALMON

Make the basic cream sauce, then add the smoked salmon, torn or cut into bite-size pieces. Add the chopped dill and stir. Season with some salt and black pepper.

SPINACH

Make the basic cream sauce, then roughly chop and add the baby spinach. Cook, stirring constantly, over low heat for 1–2 minutes until the spinach has wilted. Add a pinch of nutmeg if desired.

PASTA WITH *roasted red peppers* AND GOAT CHEESE

serves 4 / preparation : 8 minutes
equipment : large saucepan, frying pan

14 oz (400 g)
marinated roasted
red peppers in oil

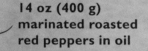

1 lb 2 oz (500 g)
fresh fettucine
or farfalle

5½ oz (150 g)
goat cheese

3 garlic cloves

Bring a large saucepan of water to a boil. Meanwhile, drain the peppers and reserve the oil. Roughly chop the peppers and crush the garlic.

Season the boiling water generously with fine sea salt, and cook the pasta according to the instructions on the package. Lightly drain, toss with some of the oil from the jar of peppers, and set aside.

Meanwhile, sauté the peppers and garlic in the frying pan over medium–high heat until aromatic and warmed through. Remove from the heat, add the cooked pasta, and gently toss, adding more oil from the jar to loosen. Serve immediately, crumbling the goat cheese over each serving.

SPAGHETTI WITH
garlicky BREADCRUMBS

serves 4 / preparation : 10 minutes
equipment : large saucepan, frying pan, small saucepan

7 oz (200 g/3 cups)
breadcrumbs

8 anchovy fillets

1 lb 2 oz (500 g)
fresh spaghetti

Chili oil or
chili flakes

4 garlic cloves

Bring a large saucepan of water to a boil. Meanwhile, roughly chop the anchovy fillets and finely slice the garlic. Generously season the boiling water with fine sea salt, and cook the pasta according to the instructions on the package. Drain and toss with olive oil. Set aside. Meanwhile, heat the frying pan and toast the breadcrumbs, shaking the pan frequently, until golden. Set aside.

In the small saucepan, heat 4 tablespoons olive oil over medium–low heat and add the anchovies and garlic. Cook until the anchovies start to melt and the garlic becomes fragrant. Pour over the breadcrumbs and stir, adding more olive oil to form a crumby mixture. Serve the pasta, sprinkled with the breadcrumb mixture and chili flakes, or drizzled with chili oil.

tuna AND CAPER PASTA

serves 4 / preparation : 10 minutes
equipment : large saucepan, colander, frying pan

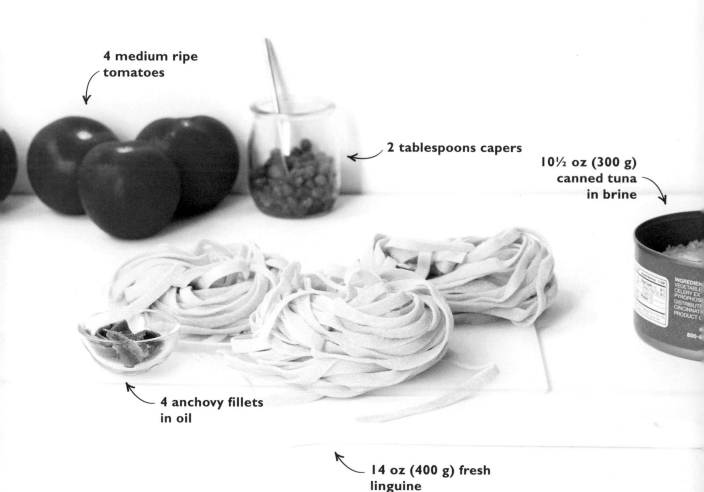

4 medium ripe tomatoes

2 tablespoons capers

10½ oz (300 g) canned tuna in brine

4 anchovy fillets in oil

14 oz (400 g) fresh linguine

Bring a large saucepan of water to a boil. Meanwhile, roughly chop the anchovy fillets and dice the tomatoes. Generously season the boiling water with fine sea salt, and cook the pasta according to the instructions on the package. Drain, reserving a little of the pasta water, toss with olive oil, and set aside.

Meanwhile, heat 2 tablespoons olive oil in the frying pan over medium heat and gently cook the anchovies until they have melted down. Turn up the heat and add the drained tuna. Cook, stirring, for 1 minute, and then add the tomatoes. Cook for a couple of minutes to warm through. Stir in the capers.

Add the cooked pasta to the frying pan with a little of the cooking water. Toss and drizzle with olive oil.

pork sausage
AND FENNEL PENNE

serves 4 / preparation : 10 minutes
equipment : large saucepan, frying pan, colander

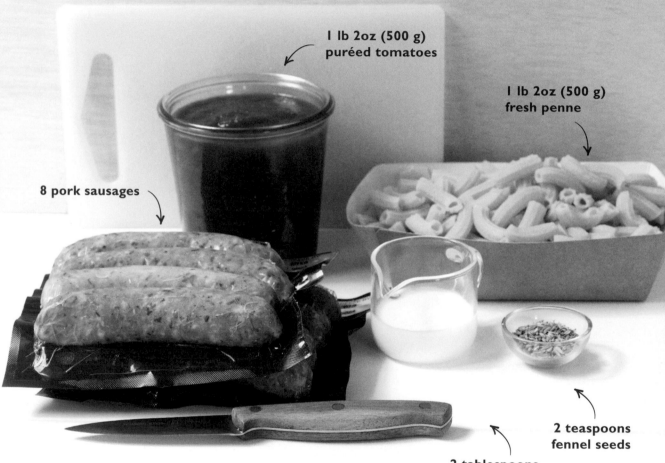

**1 lb 2oz (500 g)
puréed tomatoes**

**1 lb 2oz (500 g)
fresh penne**

8 pork sausages

**2 tablespoons
heavy cream**

**2 teaspoons
fennel seeds**

Bring a large saucepan of water to a boil, season generously with fine salt, and cook the penne according to the instructions on the package. Drain, toss with olive oil, and set aside.

Meanwhile, squeeze the sausage meat from the casings. Heat 2 tablespoons olive oil in the frying pan, add the sausage meat, breaking it up with a spoon, and cook over high heat, stirring. Drain off any liquid or fat as the meat cooks. When it starts to brown, add the fennel seeds and cook, stirring, until aromatic. Add the puréed tomatoes, stir, and cook until warmed through. Remove from the heat, stir through the cream, and season with salt and pepper. Stir the sauce through the pasta. Serve immediately with grated parmesan cheese and chopped parsley.

TORTELLINI IN *broth*

serves 4 / preparation : 5 minutes
equipment : large saucepan, vegetable peeler

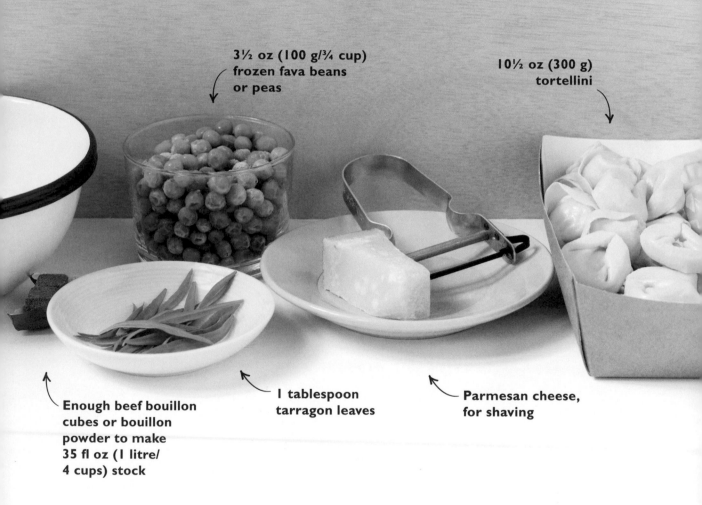

3½ oz (100 g/¾ cup)
frozen fava beans
or peas

10½ oz (300 g)
tortellini

**Enough beef bouillon
cubes or bouillon
powder to make
35 fl oz (I litre/
4 cups) stock**

**I tablespoon
tarragon leaves**

**Parmesan cheese,
for shaving**

Boil 35 fl oz (1 litre/4 cups) water in a large saucepan. Add the beef bouillon cubes or bouillon powder, and stir to dissolve over medium heat. Add the tortellini, fava beans or peas, and tarragon, and simmer for 2–3 minutes, or until the tortellini is cooked. Serve immediately with shavings of parmesan cheese scattered over each bowl.

cheesy ORZO WITH GARLIC AND BLACK PEPPER

serves 4 / preparation : 10 minutes
equipment : garlic press, cheese grater, frying pan, saucepan

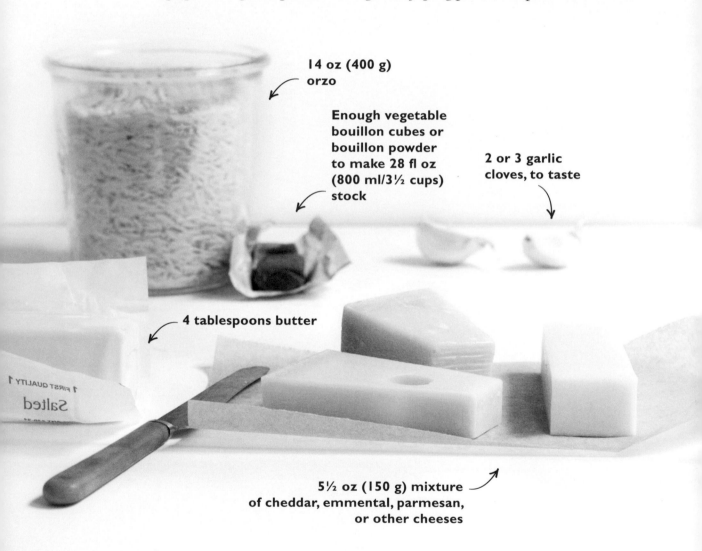

14 oz (400 g) orzo

Enough vegetable bouillon cubes or bouillon powder to make 28 fl oz (800 ml/3½ cups) stock

2 or 3 garlic cloves, to taste

4 tablespoons butter

5½ oz (150 g) mixture of cheddar, emmental, parmesan, or other cheeses

Boil 28 fl oz (800 ml/3½ cups) water in a saucepan. Meanwhile, crush the garlic and grate the cheeses. Add the orzo and bouillon cubes or powder to the boiling water and simmer for 8 minutes, stirring frequently, until cooked through and the liquid is absorbed.

Meanwhile, melt the butter in the frying pan over low heat, add the garlic, and cook gently for 3 minutes until soft and translucent. Set aside until the orzo is ready.

Add the garlicky butter, mixture of grated cheeses, and lots of freshly ground black pepper to the orzo. Stir and taste for seasoning. Serve immediately.

BASIL *pesto*

serves 2 / preparation : 5 minutes
equipment : mortar and pestle, food processor or blender, grater

**2 oz (50 g/1 cup)
basil leaves**

**A generous squeeze of
lemon, plus more to taste**

**2 oz (50 g/
⅓ cup) pine nuts**

2 garlic cloves

**2 oz (50 g)
parmesan cheese**

Place the garlic, basil, pine nuts, and a squeeze of lemon in the mortar or food processor and pound or blend to a paste. Stir in the parmesan, a bit at a time, alternating with extra virgin olive oil, to produce a smooth sauce. Add salt and pepper or more lemon juice to taste. Stir.

pesto VARIATIONS

serves 2
For something different, try one of these variations
on the Basil pesto recipe on pages 154–155

1 ½ oz (40 g/
⅓ cup)
walnuts

2 oz (60 g/
⅓ cup) toasted
almonds

1 ½ oz (40 g/
2 cups) flat-leaf
(Italian) parsley

3 oz (80 g/3 cups)
watercress

WATERCRESS AND WALNUTS

In a food processor or mortar, blend
or crush the watercress, walnuts,
1 garlic clove, and a squeeze of lemon
to a paste. Stir through 2 oz (50 g)
parmesan cheese (grated), alternating
with enough extra virgin olive oil to
produce a smooth sauce. Season.

PARSLEY AND ALMONDS

In a food processor or mortar,
blend or crush the almonds, parsley,
1 garlic clove, and a squeeze of lemon
to a coarse paste. Stir in 2 oz (50 g)
parmesan cheese (grated), alternating
with enough extra virgin olive oil to
produce a smooth sauce. Season.

2 oz (50 g/ ⅓ cup) lightly toasted hazelnuts

2 oz (50 g/2½ cups) mint leaves

2 oz (50 g/ ⅓ cup) pistachios

2 oz (50 g/2½ cups) mixed soft herbs, such as parsley, cilantro, thyme, or tarragon

MINT AND HAZELNUT PESTO

Make the basil pesto recipe on pages 154–155, but use mint leaves instead of basil, and lightly toasted hazelnuts instead of pine nuts.

PISTACHIO

Make the basil pesto recipe on pages 154–155, but use pistachios instead of pine nuts, and mixed soft herbs instead of basil.

CHAPTER 4

meat, poultry
& fish

beef carpaccio WITH
TRUFFLED MAYONNAISE

serves 4 / preparation : 5 minutes
equipment : plastic wrap

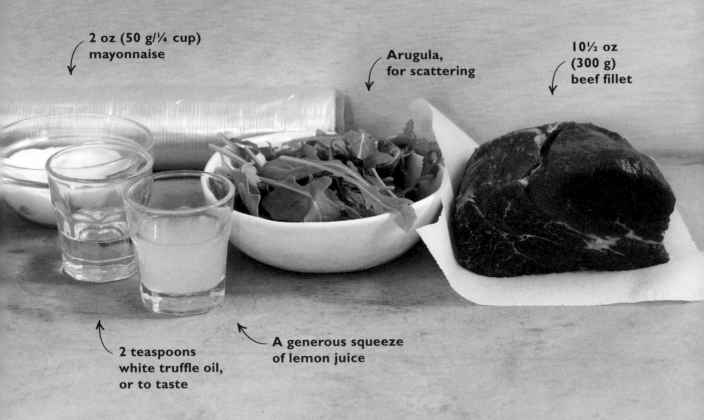

2 oz (50 g/¼ cup) mayonnaise

Arugula, for scattering

10½ oz (300 g) beef fillet

2 teaspoons white truffle oil, or to taste

A generous squeeze of lemon juice

Wrap the beef tightly in plastic wrap and place in the freezer for 5 minutes. Meanwhile, mix together the mayonnaise, truffle oil, lemon juice, 2 tablespoons mild olive oil, and salt and pepper.

Cut the beef into wafer-thin slices with a very sharp knife. To make slices super thin, pound them between sheets of plastic wrap. Arrange on serving plates. Spoon the truffled mayonnaise over the top and scatter with the arugula.

STICKY *beef* STIR-FRY

serves 4 / preparation : 10 minutes
equipment : frying pan or wok

**4 tablespoons
hoisin sauce**

4 garlic cloves

**10½ oz (300 g)
rice noodles**

**9 oz (250 g)
trimmed green
beans**

**1 lb 5 oz (600 g) steak,
such as rump,
rib-eye, or sirloin**

Heat 2 tablespoons of vegetable oil in the frying pan or wok until it smokes. Meanwhile, slice the steak into thin strips and season generously with salt and pepper. Set aside.

Finely slice the garlic. Add the beans to the hot pan and stir-fry for 3 minutes. Add the meat and garlic and cook for 3 more minutes, stirring constantly. Add the noodles and hoisin and stir-fry for 1 more minute. Serve immediately.

SIZZLING SPICED *lamb* WITH HUMMUS

serves 2 / preparation : 8 minutes
equipment : frying pan, bowl, serving plate

2 tablespoons
ras el hanout

2 lamb
steaks

2 tablespoons
pine nuts

7 oz (200 g/
1 cup) hummus

2 tablespoons
honey

Set the frying pan over high heat. Meanwhile, finely chop the lamb and place in the bowl with the ras el hanout, honey, 1 tablespoon olive oil, and salt and pepper. Mix together with your hands so that all the meat is coated. Set aside. Spread the hummus onto the serving plate and make a well in the middle.

Add 1 tablespoon olive oil to the hot frying pan and add the meat. Cook, stirring occasionally, for 3–4 minutes, or until the meat is just cooked though. Spoon the meat and juices onto the hummus and scatter with the pine nuts. Garnish with flat-leaf (Italian) parsley and serve immediately with warm pita bread.

pork CHOPS AND APPLE AIOLI

serves 2 / preparation : 10 minutes
equipment : heavy frying pan, small bowl

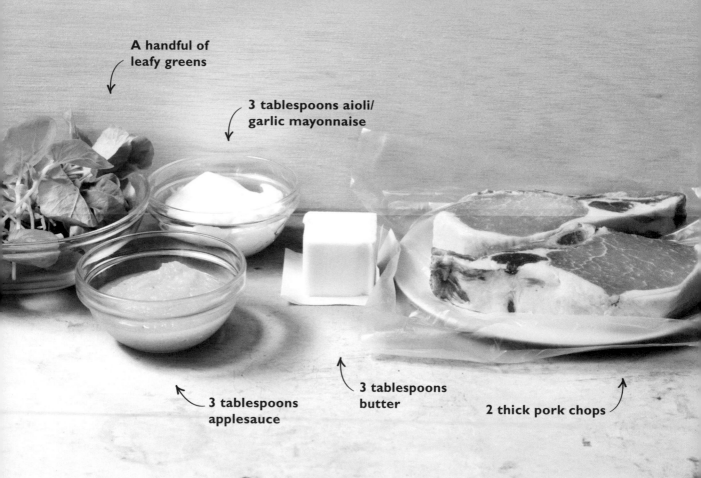

A handful of leafy greens

3 tablespoons aioli/ garlic mayonnaise

3 tablespoons applesauce

3 tablespoons butter

2 thick pork chops

Generously season the chops with salt and pepper. Set the frying pan over medium heat and melt the butter. When foaming, add the chops and cook for 4 minutes each side, or until golden and cooked through.

Meanwhile, in the small bowl, mix together the aioli and applesauce. Season with salt and pepper. Serve the pork chops with a dollop of aioli and leafy greens on the side.

liver WITH BALSAMIC MUSTARD SAUCE

serves 2 / preparation : 10 minutes
equipment : frying pan

**3 tablespoons
heavy cream**

**A handful of
watercress**

**2 tablespoons
balsamic vinegar**

**7 oz (200 g) lamb's
or calf's liver**

3 scallions

Set the frying pan over medium-high heat. Meanwhile, finely chop the white parts of the scallions and discard the green parts. Then slice the liver into strips. Place 2 tablespoons olive oil in the frying pan and add the scallions. Cook, stirring, until softened. Add the liver and fry for about 1 minute over medium heat, turning the pieces until browned on the outside and pink in the middle. Set them aside.

Increase the heat and add the balsamic vinegar. Scrape the bottom of the pan with a spoon, as it bubbles up, and cook for about 30 seconds. Reduce the heat to medium and add the cream and mustard, stirring constantly, until warmed through and thickened. Season with salt and pepper. Drizzle the sauce over the meat and serve immediately with the watercress.

steak AND BLUE CHEESE BUTTER

serves 2 / preparation : 8 minutes
equipment : grill pan, bowl, sheet of parchment paper, foil

2 handfuls of arugula

3½ oz (100 g) blue cheese, such as Gorgonzola or Roquefort

7 oz (200 g) unsalted butter

2 thick rib-eye steaks

Set the grill pan over high heat. Rub a little olive oil over the steaks and generously sprinkle with salt and pepper. Set aside. Mash half the butter and all of the blue cheese together in the bowl with a fork. Place in parchment paper, roll into a sausage shape, and place in the freezer.

Place the steaks on the hot pan and cook for 30 seconds on each side. Add the remaining butter and cook for 4–5 minutes more for medium–rare, turning the steaks every 30 seconds and basting them with the butter. Wrap them loosely in foil. Cut slices of the blue cheese butter and serve on top of the steak alongside a handful of arugula. Keep any leftover butter in the freezer for later use.

butter VARIATIONS

serves 2

*For something different, try one of these variations
on the Steak and blue cheese butter recipe on pages 170-171*

**4 anchovy fillets
in oil (drained
weight)**

**2 teaspoons
crushed black
peppercorns**

**1 teaspoon sea
salt flakes**

**2 teaspoons
finely chopped
rosemary**

1 garlic clove

**Finely grated zest of
2 lemons**

LEMON AND BLACK PEPPER

Mash 7 oz (200 g) softened butter
with the lemon zest, crushed black
peppercorns, and sea salt flakes.
Serve with fish, chicken, or pork.

ANCHOVY, GARLIC, ROSEMARY

Mash together 7 oz (200 g) softened
butter with the anchovy fillets (finely
chopped), rosemary, and garlic
(crushed). Serve with lamb or beef.

Each variation makes about 7 oz (200 g/¾ cup). The butter can be cut into discs, wrapped in parchment paper, and stored in the freezer for up to 4 weeks.

2 fl oz (60 ml/¼ cup) applesauce

½ teaspoon sea salt flakes

¾ oz (20 g) red chili pepper

Finely grated zest of 4 limes

I teaspoon sea salt flakes

3 teaspoons Dijon mustard

APPLE AND MUSTARD

Using an electric beater, beat together 7 oz (200 g) softened butter, the applesauce, the Dijon mustard, and the sea salt flakes. Serve with pork.

CHILI AND LIME

Mash together 7 oz (200 g) softened butter, the lime zest, red chili pepper (deseeded and finely sliced), and I teaspoon sea salt flakes. Serve with chicken, fish, and shrimp.

chicken WITH CITRUS AND THYME

serves 2 / preparation : 10 minutes
equipment : large grill pan, plastic wrap, rolling pin,
shallow bowl, lemon squeezer, small bowl, whisk

1 lemon

**12 asparagus tips
or baby asparagus
spears**

**1 large (or 2 small)
skinless, boneless
chicken breasts**

3 thyme sprigs

Set the grill pan over medium heat. Place the chicken between 2 pieces of plastic wrap and pound with the rolling pin until very thin. Place the chicken in the shallow bowl. Squeeze the lemon, pour it into the small bowl, and add the leaves from the thyme sprigs, 1 tablespoon olive oil, and salt and pepper. Whisk. Pour three-quarters of the mixture over the chicken and massage it in. Drizzle the asparagus with a little olive oil.

Place the chicken and asparagus tips or spears on the grill pan. Cook for 5 minutes, turning the chicken and asparagus every minute or so, until cooked through. Slice the chicken into strips and serve with the asparagus. Drizzle over the remaining dressing.

chicken CURRY WITH NAAN

serves 4 / preparation : 10 minutes
equipment : heavy frying pan

Naan

14 fl oz (400 ml) can coconut milk

5½ oz (150 g/ 1 cup) frozen peas

2 large skinless, boneless chicken breasts, about 1 lb 5 oz (600 g)

3 tablespoons Thai green curry paste

Preheat the oven to 350°F (180°C). Place the naan on a baking sheet and put in the oven. Heat 2 tablespoons vegetable oil in the frying pan over medium–high heat. Meanwhile, slice the chicken into very thin strips and add to the pan. Stir-fry for 3 minutes.

Add the curry paste, coconut milk, and peas and cook for 4 minutes, or until the chicken is cooked through. Serve with warm naan.

JERK *chicken* FAJITAS

serves 4 / preparation : 10 minutes
equipment : grill pan, shallow bowl, tongs

1 red bell pepper

1 red onion

4 flour tortillas

2 teaspoons jerk spice

2 skinless, boneless chicken breasts

Set the grill pan over high heat. Slice the chicken into ¼ inch (5 mm) strips and place in the bowl. Add the jerk spice, salt and pepper, and 2 teaspoons vegetable oil. Mix and set aside.

Slice the onion and pepper into thin strips. Add to the chicken and mix well. Spoon the chicken and vegetables onto the hot grill pan and cook, turning constantly, for 5 minutes or until cooked through. Place the mixture in the center of the tortillas and roll up. Serve immediately with cilantro and lime wedges.

VIETNAMESE *duck* ROLLS

makes 6 rolls / preparation : 10 minutes
equipment : medium bowl, colander, large bowl filled with warm water

1 smoked
duck breast

1½ oz (40 g)
vermicelli
noodles

3 fl oz (90 ml/
⅓ cup) hoisin
sauce

3 scallions

6 Vietnamese spring
roll wrappers

Boil water in a medium pan. Meanwhile, finely slice the scallions into 4 inch (10 cm) pieces and cut the duck breast into thin strips. Place the noodles in the medium bowl, cover with boiling water, and soak for 5 minutes. Drain and rinse.

To assemble, dip each spring roll wrapper into a bowl of warm water, place on a clean work surface, and place some noodles, scallions, duck, and hoisin sauce in the center, being careful not to overfill the wrapper. Fold the bottom of the wrapper over the filling, then fold in the sides and tightly roll up. Serve immediately or cover with a damp, clean dish towel until ready to serve.

SESAME *tuna* AND NOODLES

serves 2 / preparation : 8 minutes
equipment : grill pan, saucepan, colander

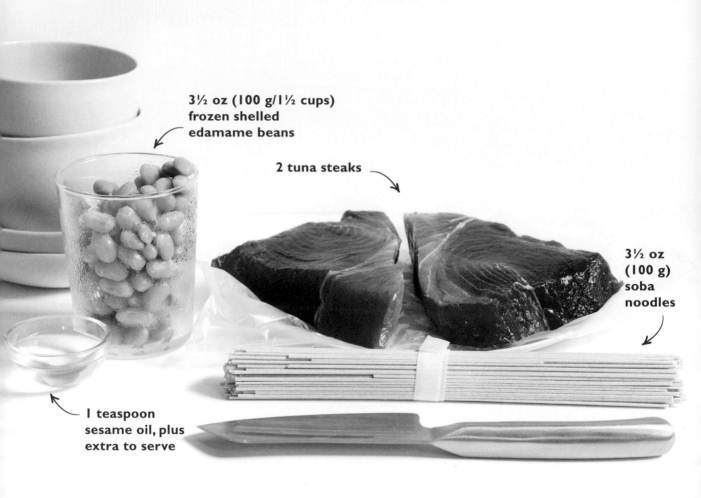

**3½ oz (100 g/1½ cups)
frozen shelled
edamame beans**

2 tuna steaks

**3½ oz
(100 g)
soba
noodles**

**1 teaspoon
sesame oil, plus
extra to serve**

Boil water in a medium pan. Meanwhile, set the grill pan over high heat. Brush the tuna with vegetable oil and generously season with freshly ground black pepper. Sear for 1 minute on each side and set aside. Cook the noodles in the boiling water according to the instructions on the package. Add the edamame beans 2 minutes before the end of cooking. Drain, rinse under cold water, and return to the pan. Toss with the sesame oil.

Slice the tuna into strips and serve on top of the edamame beans and noodles. Drizzle with extra sesame oil if you like.

SMOKED *haddock* WITH HARISSA COUSCOUS

serves 4 / preparation : 10 minutes
equipment : frying pan, heatproof mixing bowl, plastic wrap

10½ oz (300 g/ 1½ cups) couscous

Enough vegetable bouillon cubes or bouillon powder to make 35 fl oz (1 litre/ 4 cups) stock

14 oz (400 g) smoked haddock or mackerel fillets

A handful of cilantro leaves

1 tablespoon harissa paste

Boil water in a medium pan. Meanwhile, roughly chop the cilantro and set the frying pan over high heat. Pour 35 fl oz (1 litre/4 cups) of the boiling water into the mixing bowl, mix in the bouillon cube or bouillon powder, and add the couscous. Stir, cover with plastic wrap, and set aside for 5 minutes. Meanwhile, add 2 tablespoons vegetable oil to the frying pan and cook the fish for 2 minutes each side.

When the couscous is done, fluff up with a fork and stir through the harissa paste and cilantro. Add salt and pepper to taste. Serve with the smoked haddock flaked over the top. Discard the skin.

sea bass IN DASHI BROTH

serves 2 / preparation : 8 minutes
equipment : pastry brush, small saucepan, frying pan, spatula, 2 shallow soup bowls

Enough dashi granules, fish bouillon cubes or bouillon powder to make 17 fl oz (500 ml/2 cups) stock

2 handfuls of baby spinach

2 sea bass fillets, skin on

1 tablespoon soy sauce

4 scallions

Boil 17 fl oz (500 ml/2 cups) water in a small saucepan. Meanwhile, pat the fish dry and score the skin. Brush both sides with vegetable oil and generously season with salt and pepper. Set aside.

Add the dashi and soy to the boiling water in the saucepan. Finely slice the scallions and add them to the pan. Keep warm over low heat. Heat the frying pan over high heat and cook the fish fillets, skin-side down, for 3–4 minutes. Carefully turn over and cook for 1–2 minutes more. Place a handful of spinach in each bowl and pour in enough broth to cover. Place a fish fillet on top and serve immediately.

GRILLED *herring* AND PICKLED CUCUMBERS

serves 2 / preparation : 10 minutes
equipment : grill pan, vegetable peeler, bowl, pastry brush

1 cucumber, about 14 oz (400 g)

2 tablespoons rice wine vinegar

4 whole herring, cleaned

1 heaping teaspoon superfine sugar

Set the grill pan over high heat. Meanwhile, peel the cucumber and slice into ribbons with the vegetable peeler. Place in the bowl and add the vinegar, sugar, a pinch of chili flakes (if using), and ¼ teaspoon sea salt flakes. Set aside.

Sparingly brush the herring with olive oil and sprinkle with salt and pepper. Cook for 3–5 minutes on the grill pan, turning every minute or so, until cooked through. Serve immediately with the pickled cucumbers and lemon wedges.

SALT AND PEPPER *calamari*

serves 2 / preparation : 10 minutes
equipment : large saucepan, large plate, paper towels, slotted spoon

Lemon wedges

1 ½ oz (40 g) cornstarch

9 oz (250 g) squid rings

Pour enough vegetable oil into the saucepan to come 1¼ inches (3 cm) up the sides. Set over high heat. Meanwhile, spread the cornstarch on the large plate and add 1 teaspoon sea salt flakes and 2 teaspoons ground black pepper. Stir to combine. Toss the squid rings in the cornstarch mixture. When the oil is very hot—a small piece of bread should turn golden brown in 30 seconds—cook the squid in batches until golden, maximum 1 minute per batch.

Transfer the calamari to paper towels with a slotted spoon. Serve immediately with a squeeze of lemon.

shrimp AND NOODLE SATAY

serves 4 / preparation : 10 minutes
equipment : wok or large frying pan, small bowl

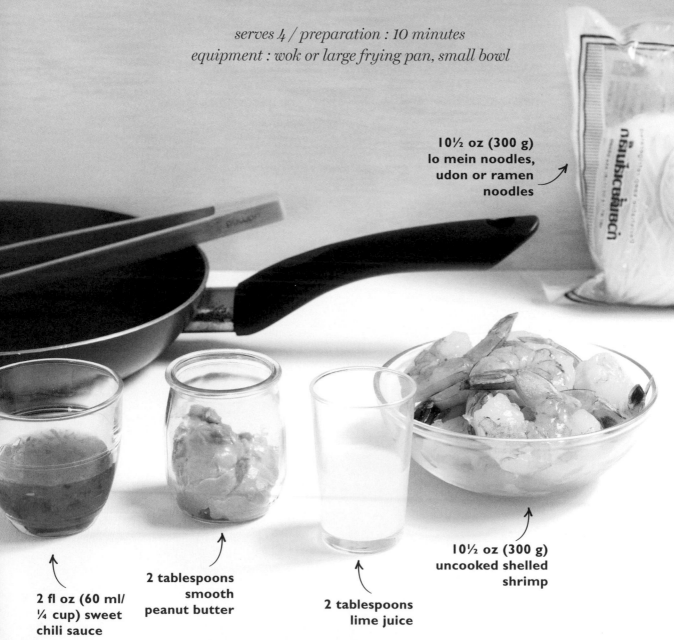

10½ oz (300 g) lo mein noodles, udon or ramen noodles

10½ oz (300 g) uncooked shelled shrimp

2 fl oz (60 ml/ ¼ cup) sweet chili sauce

2 tablespoons smooth peanut butter

2 tablespoons lime juice

Heat the wok or frying pan over medium–high heat. In the small bowl, mix the peanut butter, chili sauce, and lime juice. Set aside.

Add 2 tablespoons vegetable oil to the wok or frying pan and add the shrimp. Stir-fry for 1 minute over high heat until the shrimp are just pink. Add the noodles and sauce, and toss until the noodles are warmed through and coated with sauce. Add a splash of water to loosen if necessary. Season with salt and black pepper and serve immediately with lime wedges.

calamari, CHORIZO, AND ALMOND SALAD

serves 4 as a main / preparation : 10 minutes
equipment : shallow bowl, salad bowl, frying pan, slotted spoon

10½ oz (300 g) chorizo

1 lb 5 oz (600 g) squid tentacles, cleaned and halved

A handful of arugula

1 lemon

¾ oz (20 g/ ¼ cup) sliced almonds

Rinse the squid tentacles and pat them dry. Place the squid in the bowl, squeeze over half of the lemon, drizzle with olive oil, and season with salt and pepper. Toss and set aside. In the frying pan, heat 1 tablespoon olive oil over medium–high heat. Thinly slice the chorizo and fry until it starts to crisp. Transfer to the salad bowl with the slotted spoon.

Turn the heat to high, add the squid, and stir-fry for about 3 minutes until tender and just cooked through. Transfer to the salad bowl with the pan juices. Add the arugula, squeeze over the remaining half lemon, drizzle with extra virgin olive oil, and season with salt and pepper. Toss. Serve, sprinkled with the almonds.

FISH EN *papillote*

serves 2 / preparation : 10 minutes
equipment : 2 large rectangles of parchment paper, baking sheet

A splash of
white wine

4 tablespoons
heavy cream

2 very thin fish fillets
(cod, haddock, sea bream,
sea bass, or salmon)

A handful of soft
herbs such as parsley,
tarragon, or dill

Preheat the oven to 450°F (230°C). Place each fish fillet on a piece of parchment paper. Spoon the cream over the fillets, season with salt and pepper, and scatter with herbs. Fold the paper over and scrunch the edges together to make a parcel, leaving a small opening. Pour in the wine, then seal tightly, leaving room for the parcel to expand. Place on the baking sheet and bake for 8 minutes. Serve in the paper with lemon wedges and extra salt.

FISH *en papillote*
VARIATIONS

serves 2

*For something different, try one of these variations on the basic
Fish en papillote recipe on pages 196–197*

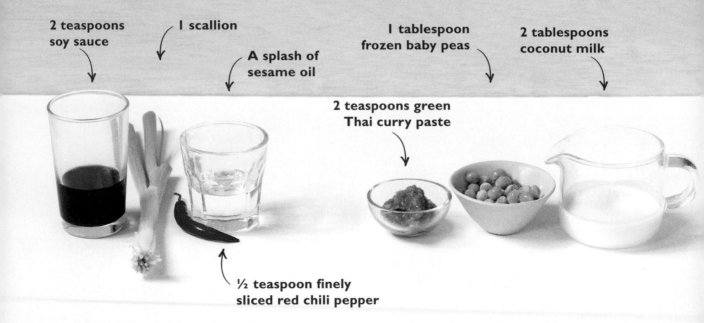

2 teaspoons
soy sauce

I scallion

A splash of
sesame oil

I tablespoon
frozen baby peas

2 tablespoons
coconut milk

2 teaspoons green
Thai curry paste

½ teaspoon finely
sliced red chili pepper

SOY SAUCE AND SCALLIONS

To each fish parcel add soy sauce,
scallion, sesame oil, and red chili
pepper.

THAI CURRY

To each fish parcel add green Thai
curry paste, frozen baby peas, and
coconut milk.

**2 tablespoons
puréed tomatoes**

**A handful of
watercress leaves**

**I teaspoon chopped
tarragon**

**A pinch
of dried
oregano**

**I tablespoon
chopped black
olives**

TOMATO AND OLIVES

To each fish parcel add puréed
tomatoes, black olives, and dried
oregano.

WATERCRESS AND TARRAGON

To each fish parcel add watercress
leaves and tarragon.

CHAPTER 5

sweet things

CHOCOLATE *cherry* TRUFFLES

makes 28 / preparation : 6 minutes
equipment : food processor

A pinch of salt

5½ oz (150 g) chocolate sandwich cookies

1½ oz (40 g/¼ cup) dried cherries or cranberries

1½ oz (40 g/¼ cup) cream cheese

Place all the ingredients in the food processor and process until smooth.

Roll level teaspoonfuls of the mixture into balls. Serve immediately or chill until ready to serve.

Serve dusted with cocoa powder if you like.

WHITE *chocolate* BITES

makes 16 / preparation : 5 minutes + 20 to 30 minutes chilling
equipment : saucepan and a heatproof bowl that will sit on top of it, mixing bowl,
baking sheet lined with parchment paper

7 oz (200 g) granola, ideally one with lots of dried fruit

9 oz (250 g) white chocolate

Fill a saucepan with water and bring it to a boil. Meanwhile, break the chocolate into small pieces and place in the heatproof bowl. Sit the bowl of chocolate on top of the boiling water in the saucepan and cook over low heat, stirring, until it has melted.

Combine the melted chocolate and granola in the mixing bowl and stir until thoroughly combined. Place tablespoons of the mixture onto the lined baking sheet, then chill for about 20–30 minutes until set.

goodness BARS

makes 12 bars / preparation : 5 minutes
equipment : food processor or blender, 5 x 9 inch (13 x 23 cm) cake pan

4 oz (120 g/
1¼ cups)
rolled oats

3½ oz (100 g/½ cup)
dried apricots

2 oz (50 g/2 cups)
puffed rice

4 tablespoons peanut
butter (or other
nut butter)

2½ fl oz (75 ml/
⅓ cup) honey

Put the oats in the food processor or blender and grind to a powder. Add the peanut butter, honey, apricots, and puffed rice, and process until the mixture forms a ball.

Press the mixture into a pan and cut into bar shapes measuring about 2½ inches (6 cm) long and ¾ inch (2 cm) wide.

TOFFEE *popcorn*

serves 4 as a snack / preparation : 8 minutes + 5 minutes cooling
equipment : small saucepan, large heavy lidded saucepan,
non-stick baking sheet

**3 tablespoons
golden syrup or
light corn syrup**

**2 oz (50 g/¼ cup)
popcorn kernels**

**2 tablespoons
salted butter**

Melt the syrup and butter in the small pan with some salt. Simmer vigorously for 1 minute, then remove from the heat.

Pour the popcorn into the large pan and add 1 tablespoon vegetable oil. Stir to coat, then cover and set over medium–high heat. When the first kernel pops, remove the pan from the heat for 1 minute, covered, then return to the heat. Frequently shake the pan as the kernels pop. When the popping slows down, remove the pan from the heat for 1 minute, with the lid on. Add the syrup mixture, stirring well to coat. Spread the popcorn on the baking sheet to cool.

NO-BAKE *peanut* BUTTER COOKIES

makes 24 / preparation : 10 minutes + 10 minutes cooling
equipment : saucepan, large sheet of parchment paper

8½ oz (235 g/
1½ cups) rolled
oats

2 fl oz (60 ml/
¼ cup) milk

2 oz (55 g/
¼ cup)
unsalted
buter

8 oz (225 g/
1 cup) sugar

2 tablespoons
peanut butter

Place the sugar, butter, milk, and a generous pinch of fine sea salt in the pan and cook, stirring, over medium–low heat until the sugar dissolves. Increase the heat to medium and boil, stirring constantly, for 2 minutes.

Remove the pan from the heat and add the oats and peanut butter. Stir until combined. Return the pan to the heat and cook for 1 more minute, stirring constantly. Working quickly, use 2 spoons to drop tablespoonfuls of the mixture onto the parchment paper. Flatten the mixture with the back of a spoon to form cookie shapes. The cookies will harden as they cool.

SUGAR AND *spice* CROUSTILLANTS

makes 8 / preparation : 10 minutes + 5 minutes cooling
equipment : mixing bowl, 2 sheets parchment paper, baking sheet lined with parchment paper

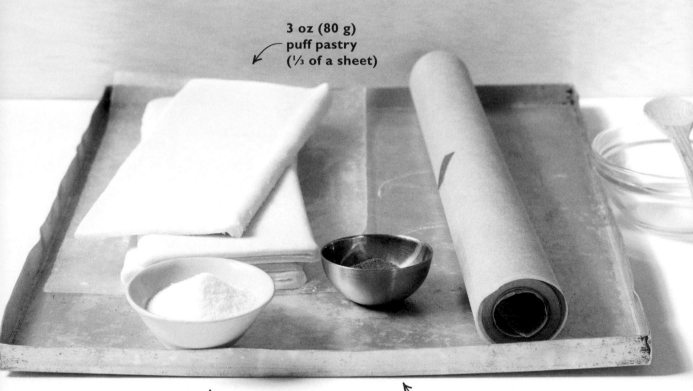

3 oz (80 g) puff pastry (⅓ of a sheet)

1 ½ tablespoons sugar

1 tablespoon mixed spices (cinnamon, nutmeg, allspice, etc)

Preheat the oven to 400°F (200°C). Combine the sugar and mixed spices in the bowl.

Cut the pastry into 8 rectangles. Roll out 4 pieces at a time between 2 sheets of parchment paper to make long rectangles. Transfer the pastry to the lined baking sheet.

Prick the pastry all over with a fork and sprinkle with the sugar mixture. Bake the croustillants for 6–7 minutes or until golden brown. Serve warm.

MARSHMALLOW *chocolate* S'MORES

makes 4 / preparation : 5 minutes
equipment : baking sheet lined with parchment paper

8 Graham crackers or speculaas cookies

3 oz (80 g) marshmallow fluff or about 8 large marshmallows

1½ oz (40 g) milk chocolate squares

Turn on the broiler. Place 4 Graham crackers or speculaas on the lined baking sheet and distribute the chocolate equally on each. Top with marshmallow fluff or marshmallows. Cook for about 2 minutes, or until the marshmallow is browned. Place a Graham cracker or speculaas cookie on top of each and serve immediately.

figs WITH CARAMEL CREAM AND PISTACHIOS

serves 2 / preparation : 10 minutes
equipment : frying pan, saucepan

5 fl oz (150 ml) heavy cream

4 ripe figs

2 tablespoons unsalted butter

Pistachio nuts, for sprinkling

5½ oz (150 g) dark muscovado sugar

Cut the figs in half lengthways. Melt the butter in the frying pan and cook the figs cut-side down for 2 minutes over medium–high heat. Turn the fruit over and cook for 1 more minute. Set aside.

Combine the cream and sugar in the saucepan and gently simmer for a few minutes. Serve the figs drizzled with the caramel cream and sprinkled with pistachios.

DRIED *fruit* COMPOTE WITH RICOTTA

serves 2 / preparation : 10 minutes
equipment : 2 small saucepans, lemon squeezer, slotted spoon, 2 serving bowls

9 oz (250 g) ready-to-eat soft dried fruit

3 heaping tablespoons ricotta

1 star anise or 2 cloves

1 cinnamon stick

1 lemon

Boil water in a small saucepan. Place the fruit, cinnamon, and star anise or cloves in another small saucepan. Add about 14 fl oz (400 ml/1½ cups) boiling water, or just enough to cover the fruit. Squeeze the juice from the lemon and add to the pan. Briskly simmer for 8 minutes, or longer, if time allows.

Meanwhile, beat the ricotta until creamy. When the fruit is cooked, scoop it out into serving bowls with the slotted spoon, discarding the cinnamon stick and star anise or cloves. Serve the fruit drizzled with some of the cooking liquid and a dollop of ricotta.

BASIC *cheesecake*

serves 8 / preparation : 10 minutes + 1 hour chilling
equipment : small saucepan, food processor, 20 cm (8 inch) springform
cake pan, electric beater

8 oz (220 g/ 1 cup) cream cheese

7 oz (200 g) speculaas cookies (or other spice cookies)

3½ oz (100 g) butter

10½ fl oz (300 ml/ 1¼ cups) heavy cream

2 tablespoons confectioners' sugar

Melt the butter in the pan. Meanwhile, process the speculaas in the food processor to form coarse crumbs. Add the mixture to the melted butter and stir to combine. Press firmly into the base of the cake pan. Chill the mixture while you make the filling.

Beat the cream, cream cheese, and confectioners' sugar until smooth and very thick. Spread over the cookie base and chill before releasing from the pan to serve.

cheesecake VARIATIONS

serves 8
For something different, try one of these variations on
the Basic cheesecake recipe on pages 222–223

**A few slices
of banana**

**3 tablespoons
maple syrup**

**4 tablespoons dulce
de leche**

**A few sea
salt flakes**

MAPLE AND BANANA

Make the basic cheesecake recipe, but beat the maple syrup into the cheesecake filling instead of sugar. Drizzle with more maple syrup and top with some sliced banana just before serving.

SALTED CARAMEL

Make the basic cheesecake recipe, then spread the dulce de leche over the top of the filling and lightly sprinkle with some sea salt flakes before chilling.

Finely grated zest of 2 limes

2½ fl oz (80 ml/ ⅓ cup) lime juice

7 oz (200 g) ginger cookies

9 oz (250 g/ I cup) lemon curd

7 oz (200 g) Graham crackers

Finely grated zest of I lemon

KEY LIME

Make the basic cheesecake recipe, but use Graham crackers instead of speculaas. Beat the lime juice and most of the zest into the cheesecake filling, reserving some of the zest to sprinkle over the top of the cheesecake before chilling.

LEMON

Use ginger cookies instead of speculaas to make the cheesecake base, and add lemon zest to the cheesecake filling. Spread the lemon curd over the cheesecake base just before you add the filling.

ORANGE AND *rosewater* SYLLABUB

serves 4 / preparation : 5 minutes
equipment : citrus squeezer, grater, small bowl, mixing bowl,
electric beater, 4 drinking glasses

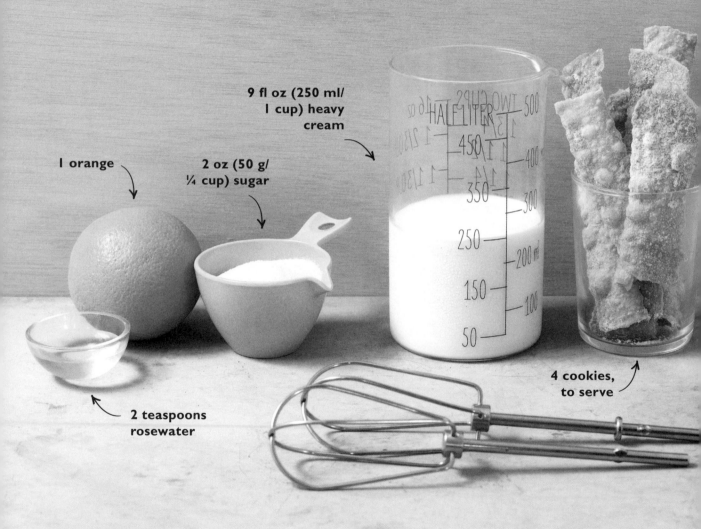

9 fl oz (250 ml/
1 cup) heavy
cream

1 orange

2 oz (50 g/
¼ cup) sugar

4 cookies,
to serve

2 teaspoons
rosewater

Squeeze the juice of the orange and finely grate the zest. Pour the juice into the small bowl, add most of the zest, the rosewater, and sugar. Stir to dissolve.

In the mixing bowl, beat the cream to soft peaks. Gradually add the orange juice mixture, beating as you go, until light and airy. Be careful not to overbeat or the cream will turn lumpy.

Spoon the mixture into the glasses, sprinkle with the remaining orange zest, and serve with the cookies.

chocolate CAKE IN A MUG

serves 1 / preparation : 5 minutes
equipment : microwaveable mug (of at least 12 fl oz/350 ml capacity), microwave

2 tablespoons self-rising flour

1 egg

2½ tablespoons sugar

2 tablespoons milk

2 tablespoons cocoa powder

Put the flour, sugar, cocoa, and egg in the mug. Whisk. Add the milk and 2 tablespoons vegetable oil. Stir until smooth.

Microwave on high for 3 minutes.

Serve dusted with confectioners' sugar if you like.

blueberry MUG CAKE

serves 1 / preparation : 5 minutes
equipment : microwaveable mug (of at least 12 fl oz/350 ml capacity), microwave

2 tablespoons milk

3 tablespoons sugar

3 tablespoons self-rising flour

1 oz (25 g/¼ cup) blueberries, plus extra to serve

1 egg

Put the flour, sugar, and egg in the mug and stir to combine. Add the milk and 2 tablespoons vegetable oil. Stir until smooth. Stir in the blueberries.

Microwave for 3 minutes on high.

Serve with extra blueberries and cream if you like.

white chocolate
AND BLUEBERRY MOUSSE

serves 4 / preparation : 8 minutes, plus 1 hour chilling
equipment : saucepan and a heatproof bowl that fits on top, electric beater,
4 ramekins or small glass bowls

9 fl oz (250 ml/
1 cup) heavy
cream

5½ oz (150 g/1 cup)
blueberries, plus extra
to serve

4½ oz (125 g/
¾ cup) white
chocolate chips

Fill the sink with ½ inch (1 cm) cold water. Fill the saucepan a quarter of the way with water and bring to a simmer. Put the chocolate and 2 tablespoons of the cream into the heatproof bowl and place it over the pan, stirring occasionally, until the chocolate has melted. Place the bowl in the sink of water to cool for a few minutes. Add the rest of the cream and beat until stiff. Fold in the blueberries.

Spoon the mousse into 4 ramekins and chill for 1 hour before serving. Serve with extra blueberries or shaved white chocolate.

TRADITIONAL *tiramisu*

serves 4 / preparation : 8 minutes
equipment : large shallow dish, 4 pretty glasses, electric beater, bowl, grater

16 ladyfingers

**13 oz (375 g/1½ cups)
mascarpone cheese**

**6 fl oz (180 ml/
¾ cup) cold
espresso or
5 teaspoons
instant coffee**

**Dark chocolate,
for sprinkling**

**2 tablespoons
sugar**

If using instant coffee, stir well into 6 fl oz (180 ml/¾ cup) cold water. Break each ladyfinger into 4 pieces and place in the shallow dish. Cover with the cold coffee, gently turning the pieces over. Set aside. Beat the mascarpone with the sugar and 3½ fl oz (100 ml/⅓ cup) cold water.

Carefully distribute half of the soaked ladyfingers among the glasses. Spread half the mascarpone mixture over the top, then add the remaining ladyfingers. Finish with a layer of the remaining mascarpone mixture. Top with lots of grated chocolate. Serve immediately or chill to let the flavors combine.

tiramisu VARIATIONS

serves 4

*For something different, try one of these variations. Make the
Traditional tiramisu on pages 232–233, but ...*

10 fl oz
(280 ml/
1¼ cups)
pomegranate
juice

7 fl oz (200 ml/¾ cup)
syrup from a can of
lychees

I teaspoon rosewater

A handful of
pomegranate
seeds

A few canned
lychees

POMEGRANATE

... use 6 fl oz (180 ml/¾ cup)
pomegranate juice to pour over the
lady fingers instead of espresso, and
3½ fl oz (100 ml/⅓ cup) pomegranate
juice in the mascarpone mixture, instead
of water. Add pomegranate seeds to
the layers, finishing with pomegranate
seeds instead of grated chocolate.

LYCHEE AND ROSEWATER

... use the syrup from the can of
lychees mixed with the rosewater
to soak the ladyfingers, and add a few
drops of rosewater to the mascarpone
cream. Add the canned lychees
(chopped) to the layers, finishing with
lychees instead of chocolate.

MARSALA

... combine the marsala, water, and sugar in a small pan. Simmer, stirring, until dissolved. Soak the ladyfingers in the mixture, instead of espresso, and beat a splash of marsala into the mascarpone cream. Add the canned peaches (chopped) to the layers, finishing with peaches, instead of chocolate.

5½ fl oz (160 ml/ ⅔ cup) marsala

2 tablespoons sugar

2 tablespoons water

5½ fl oz (160 ml/ ⅔ cup) limoncello

2 tablespoons water

A few canned peaches

A handful of blueberries

2½ tablespoons sugar

LIMONCELLO AND BLUEBERRIES

... combine the limoncello, water, and sugar in a small pan. Simmer, stirring, for a few minutes, until dissolved. Soak the ladyfingers in the mixture, instead of espresso, and beat a splash of limoncello into the mascarpone cream. Add the blueberries to the layers, finishing with blueberries, instead of chocolate.

chocolate POTS

serves 4 / preparation: 6 minutes, plus 30 minutes chilling
equipment : saucepan, small bowl, whisk, 4 ramekins

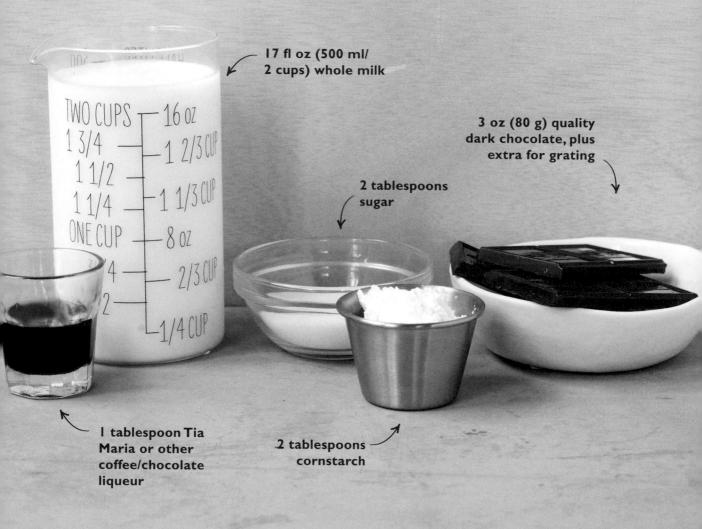

17 fl oz (500 ml/ 2 cups) whole milk

3 oz (80 g) quality dark chocolate, plus extra for grating

2 tablespoons sugar

1 tablespoon Tia Maria or other coffee/chocolate liqueur

2 tablespoons cornstarch

Heat the milk and sugar in the saucepan and remove from the heat just before the mixture starts to boil. Off the heat, break the chocolate into pieces, add it to the saucepan with the Tia Maria, and stir until just melted.

Place the cornstarch in the small bowl and add a couple tablespoons of the chocolate mixture. Stir to remove any lumps, then gradually pour the mixture into the chocolate pan, whisking as you go. Cook over gentle heat, whisking, until thick. Pour into ramekins and chill. Top with grated dark chocolate and serve with biscotti, if you like.

CARAMELIZED *oranges* WITH MAPLE CREAM

serves 2 / preparation : 5 minutes
equipment : large frying pan, electric beater, small bowl, spatula

5 fl oz (150 ml/ ⅔ cup) heavy cream

2 big oranges

1 tablespoon maple syrup

1 teaspoon ground cinnamon

2 oz (50 g/¼ cup) light muscovado or soft brown sugar

Set the frying pan over medium-high heat. Cut the skin from the oranges, removing all the pith, and cut each one into 6 slices.

Beat the cream and maple syrup together until thick. Mix together the sugar and cinnamon in the small bowl.

Cook the orange slices in the hot pan for 1 minute. Flip them over, sprinkle with the sugar and cinnamon mixture, and cook for 1 minute. Flip the orange slices over again and cook for 1 final minute, or until the sugar is bubbling. Serve hot with a spoonful of maple cream.

Eton MESS

serves 4 / preparation : 8 minutes
equipment : food processor, large bowl, electric beater

**10½ fl oz
(300 ml/1¼ cups)
heavy cream**

**14 oz (400 g)
strawberries**

**2½ oz (75 g)
meringue nests**

**2–3 tablespoons
confectioners' sugar**

Hull the strawberries. Place half in the food processor, add 1 tablespoon of the sugar, and blend to a smooth sauce. Quarter the remaining strawberries. In the bowl, whip the cream with the remaining 1–2 tablespoons sugar to form soft peaks. Don't overbeat. Crumble the meringues and fold them into the cream. Gently fold in most of the strawberry sauce and most of the chopped strawberries.

Serve drizzled with the remaining strawberry sauce and topped with the rest of the strawberries.

CHOCOLATE *brioche* TOAST

serves 4 / preparation : 6 minutes
equipment : heavy frying pan, spatula

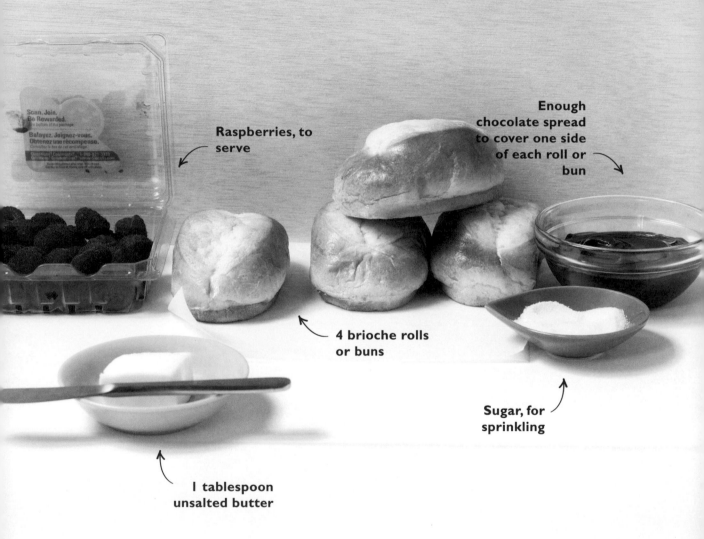

Raspberries, to serve

Enough chocolate spread to cover one side of each roll or bun

4 brioche rolls or buns

Sugar, for sprinkling

1 tablespoon unsalted butter

Cut the brioches in half. Generously spread one side with chocolate spread and then close up the halves.

Heat the butter over medium–high heat until foaming, then add the brioches. Cook for 1 minute on each side, or until golden, pressing down gently with the spatula. Serve hot, sprinkled with sugar. Enjoy the raspberries on the side.

raspberry SHERBET

serves 4 / preparation : 2 minutes
equipment : blender or food processor

3 generous tablespoons
honey, or more to taste

14 oz (400 g/
3 cups) frozen
raspberries

4½ oz (125 g/
½ cup) mascarpone
cheese

2 tablespoons
plain yogurt

Place all the ingredients together in the blender or food processor and blend until smooth, scraping down the sides frequently to get the fruit moving. Serve immediately. Alternatively, freeze the mixture until ready to eat, and blend again just before serving.

mojito GRANITA

serves 4 / preparation: 10 minutes + 4 to 6 hours
equipment : small saucepan, grater, blender, strainer, metal loaf pan

3½ oz (100 g/½ cup)
sugar

2 limes

A large handful of
mint leaves

1 ½ tablespoons
white rum

Finely grate the lime zest and place it in the saucepan with the sugar and 10½ fl oz (300 ml) water. Simmer until the sugar is dissolved. Let the syrup cool for a few minutes.

Meanwhile, squeeze the juice from the limes and place in the blender with the mint leaves, rum, and cooled sugar syrup. Process until the mint is finely chopped. Strain into the loaf pan and freeze. Scrape the mixture every hour with a fork until it resembles snow. Serve with lime slices, if you like.

FROZEN *fruit* SORBET

serves 4 / preparation : 3 minutes
equipment : food processor or blender

Place all the frozen fruit, maple syrup, and lime in the food processor or blender with some mint, if you like, and blend to the consistency of snow. Add more lime juice or maple syrup to taste.

1 lb (450 g) mixed frozen fruit such as melon, pineapple, mango, and papaya

1–2 tablespoons maple syrup, according to taste

A squeeze of lime, according to taste

CHEWY *caramel* ICE CREAM

serves 4 / preparation : 5 minutes + 2 hours freezing
equipment : mixing bowl, 2 large ice cube trays (about 48 cubes),
food processor or blender

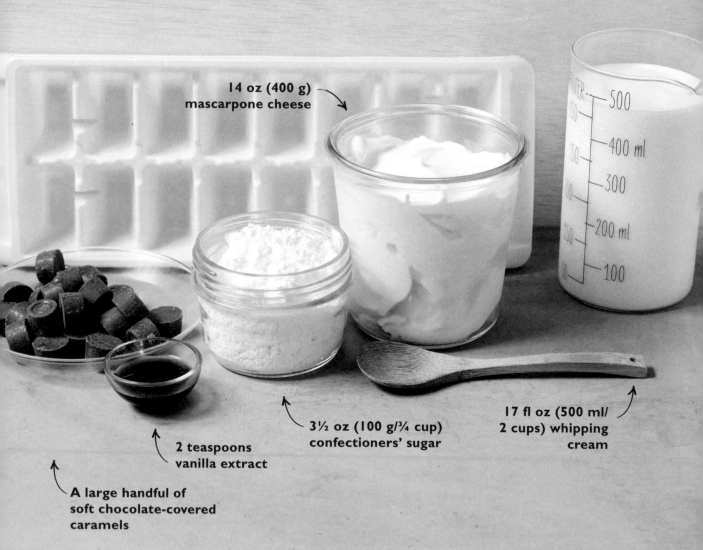

14 oz (400 g)
mascarpone cheese

2 teaspoons
vanilla extract

3½ oz (100 g/¾ cup)
confectioners' sugar

17 fl oz (500 ml/
2 cups) whipping
cream

A large handful of
soft chocolate-covered
caramels

Place the mascarpone, cream, vanilla, and confectioners' sugar in the mixing bowl and beat by hand until smooth and creamy. Scrape into the ice cube trays and freeze for about 1–2 hours.

Place the frozen ice cream cubes into the food processor or blender, add the caramels, and blend to desired consistency. Serve immediately.

lemon AND RASPBERRY JELLO

serves 4 / preparation: 10 minutes + several hours chilling
equipment : small bowl, small saucepan, 4 small jars

**3½ fl oz (100 ml)
orange juice**

**2 oz (65 g/¼ cup)
sugar**

**3½ oz (100 g/1¼ cups)
raspberries**

**6 sheets of
gelatin**

**4 fl oz (120 ml/½ cup)
lemon juice**

Boil water in a small pan. Place the gelatin sheets in the small bowl, cover with cold water, and let them soak for 3 minutes, until softened.

Meanwhile, place the sugar and 2 fl oz (65 ml/¼ cup) boiling water into the small saucepan and stir over medium heat for 1 minute or so, until dissolved. Remove from the heat, add the lemon and orange juice, and stir. Squeeze the excess water from the gelatin and add to the pan along with 7 fl oz (200 ml/¾ cup) just-boiled water. Stir until the gelatin is dissolved.

Distribute the raspberries among the jars and pour over the jello mixture. Chill for several hours until set.

INDEX

STERLING EPICURE
New York

An Imprint of Sterling Publishing Co., Inc.
1166 Avenue of the Americas
New York, NY 10036

This Sterling Epicure edition published in 2018
First Published in 2016 in France by Marabout

ISBN 978-1-4549-3059-4

Distributed in Canada by Sterling Publishing Co., Inc.
c/o Canadian Manda Group, 664 Annette Street
Toronto, Ontario M6S 2C8, Canada

For information about custom editions, special sales, and premium and corporate purchases,
please contact Sterling Special Sales at 800-805-5489 or specialsales@sterlingpublishing.com.

Manufactured in China

2 4 6 8 10 9 7 5 3 1

sterlingpublishing.com

Photography by Deirdre Rooney